BK 266.023 S9150
ON THE GROWING EDGE OF THE CHURCH
1965 .00 FV

D0936011

3000 075514 3001⁨⁩

St. Louis Community College

266.023 S9150
STREET
ON THE GROWING EDGE OF THE CHURCH
1.95

JUNIOR COLLEGE DISTRICT
of St. Louis - St. Louis County
LIBRARY

5545 West Park
St. Louis, Missouri 63105

PRINTED IN U.S.A.

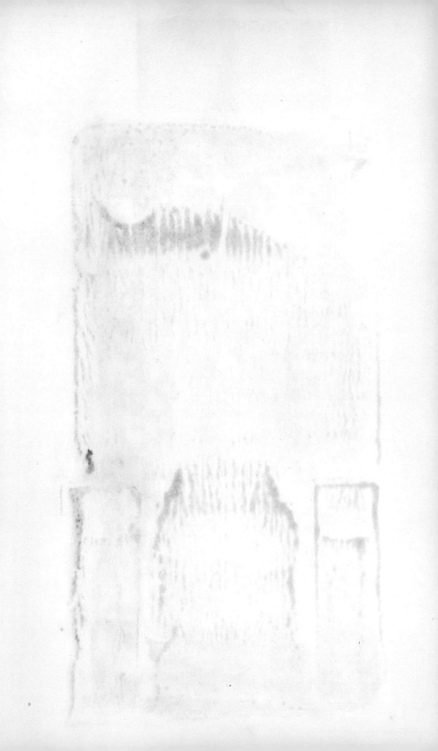

ON THE GROWING EDGE OF THE CHURCH

ON THE
GROWING EDGE
OF THE CHURCH

T. WATSON STREET

JOHN KNOX PRESS

Richmond, Virginia

Unless otherwise indicated, Scripture quotations are from the Revised Standard Version, copyright 1946 and 1952 by the Division of Christian Education of the National Council of the Churches of Christ in the United States of America.

Library of Congress Catalog Card Number: 65-12917
© M. E. Bratcher, 1965
Printed in the United States of America

2642

To colleagues on the Staff of the Board of World Missions, Presbyterian Church, U. S.

PREFACE

These few chapters are written for Christian laymen and in behalf of the growing edge of the church. While the focus of these chapters is overseas the concern for missions is needed at home and abroad, in every geographical area, indeed in every aspect of the church's life.

This writing owes most to my family. My wife, Sara Crews Street, and children helped by their interest, Have you done another chapter? and by their impatience, When will you finish? They bore heavier responsibilities at home, and gave up some family outings away from home, so I could read and study and write.

I am indebted to fellow laborers in the missionary enterprise of the Presbyterian Church, U. S., especially to the commissioned missionaries of that church. For they are at work on the growing edge of the church, and communicated to me their concern for "regions beyond" and for the people in such regions and all over the world.

This writing was done at odd times and in erratic ways. The labors of my secretary, Miss Mattye Bond, and of Mrs. J. R. Arnold and Mrs. R. B. Flathe made it possible to submit this manuscript to the publisher.

Chapters I, II, and III were delivered as lectures on the Settles Foundation at Austin Presbyterian Theological Seminary, and Chapter III formed the substance of a lecture to the Society of Theological Inquiry at Columbia Theological Seminary.

T. Watson Street
Nashville, Tennessee

CONTENTS

CONTENTS

I

The Readiness of the World
for the Gospel

Recent Japanese history gives an illustration of a conviction which has persisted in the Christian Church. The defeat of Japan in World War II was followed by the American occupation. The defeat and the occupation made possible the resumption of missionary work by American churches. These churches did more than take up once again the labors interrupted by the war. Each church made a forceful presentation to its own members of the great new opportunity in Japan, until the voices of the several churches appeared to become one united appeal with the same basic emphasis. Japanese militarism had been overcome; the old state Shinto religion had been abolished, and there was opportunity for religious change; resistance to the penetration from the West, including that of churches, had been broken and had been replaced by a new receptivity; democracy had been established. All of these factors were cited as evidence of an unparalleled opportunity for Christian missions in Japan. They added up to the readiness of Japan for the gospel. Christian response to that readiness was the urgent task of the hour. Two thousand missionaries were needed.

The church has always believed in the readiness of the world for the gospel. The meaning of that readiness has been variously interpreted. Failure to win the world for Christ has regularly been attributed not to the lack of the readiness of the world but to the failure of the church to undertake the task. The belief in this readiness has been a powerful dynamic in missionary advance. It has been a basic factor in the missionary call for many people. Missionaries have been moved not only by conviction of need but by the certainty of opportunity and of open doors. The belief that fields are white unto the harvest has motivated the inauguration of Christian work in new lands and in new areas. In like manner, the presentation of the readiness of the world for the gospel has been a favorite and powerful theme in missionary promotion. Missionary addresses and appeals made frequent reference to it. It was used to inspire missionary vision and enthusiasm and support in the home church. This certainty about readiness has not only been a powerful one; it also has been and remains a very legitimate conviction. The church has been correct in this conviction, although particular interpretations and appeals have been shallow and have included an optimism not justified by the facts of human nature and history. In a very real sense the world is always ready for the gospel.

The emphasis on the readiness of the world for the gospel was prominent in the modern missionary movement of the last two centuries. That movement made much of the coming of the "fullness of time" in certain periods and in certain areas. The "fullness of time" was seen as involving two conditions. One of these consisted of external factors. The situation in Japan can serve as an illustration. Whereas for years Japanese militarism and anti-Western feeling prevented a missionary advance led by Western churches, the defeat of Japan in World War II removed those obstacles and opened doors once closed. The readiness of a particular nation for the gospel was at times seen as the result of a change of rulers or political views, or improvement in economic conditions. At times the acquisition of a colony by a Protestant country or the expansion of a Western empire provided new opportunities. The exploration of a large island or the opening up of the vast interior of a great continent made possible the carrying of the gospel to new areas. The readiness was found at times in social gains, such as when slavery was outlawed or child labor was ended. These external factors could include advance in navigation, or progress in printing, or new knowledge of a language.

But the readiness was always interpreted as including more than external factors. It was more frequently viewed in terms of the human heart. Appeals were based primarily on a firm conviction about and a dramatic description of the conscious hunger of the human spirit. Faraway lands were pictured as longing for more and more missionaries. There was emphasis on the restless and conscious desire of the "heathen" to hear the Christian message. "Fields white unto the harvest" meant people ready and willing to enter the Christian fold, if only the opportunity were provided. A story frequently repeated told of a question on the lips of people of various tribes and tongues: Why did you wait so long? Dr. Samuel McPheeters Glasgow used that question as the basis of a hymn.

> Long have we sought eternal life,
> Years have we waited in sin and strife;
> In darkness groped, sad misery's mate,
> How long, how long must we wait?

> The aged faint and long for the Friend,
> Dark shadows gathering bring the end;
> Fades now the light, 'tis growing late,
> How long, how long must we wait?

This same note is found in one of the most widely used mission hymns, written in 1819 by Bishop Reginald Heber.

> From Greenland's icy mountains,
> From India's coral strand,
> Where Afric's sunny fountains
> Roll down their golden sand;
> From many an ancient river,
> From many a palmy plain,
> They call us to deliver
> Their land from error's chain.

These two factors—the external situation and the hunger of the human heart—figured strongly in the conviction of the modern missionary movement about the readiness of the world for the gospel. Both are illustrated in the view of the non-Christian religions. In 1928, at the time of the Jerusalem meeting of the International Missionary Conference, there was genuine optimism about the triumph of the gospel over the great non-Christian systems of life and thought. The lands of those religions were now open to the gospel. The adherents of those religions recognized the evil and the emptiness of their faith and were breaking free. They longed for the real Saviour. This was taking place at a time when the bondage of those lands and religions was being broken by outside forces. The result was a readiness for the gospel in those lands and among those peoples.

In short, modern missions have been marked by an optimism with respect to external factors and to the hunger of the human heart. They have advanced in part out of a firm conviction about the "'fullness of time." They believed that God in His providence had ordered modern progress so that mission advance could take place, and that circumstances were favorable for that advance. They believed that God had planted a hunger, frequently expressed, for the true Saviour.

We must admit that conviction on both of these points is now greatly weakened. There appears to be lacking today a deep certainty about the readiness of the world for the gospel. It would be difficult to determine all the reasons for this diminishing optimism. The mood has been affected by recent experiences in the Republic of the Congo, the expulsion of missionaries from Indonesia and other places, and numerous other events. The anti-Western, anti-white character of many of the revolutions of our time have created difficulties for many missionaries. All these events are but recent examples of developments that have been going on for decades. Since 1914, the date set by Dr. Kenneth Scott Latourette as the beginning of the "Advance Through Storm" era, there have taken place two world wars, rampaging nationalism, world revolution, the movement for independence in countries all over the world, and the spread of Communism.

A great blow to our confidence about the readiness of the world for the gospel came in the loss of China. The loss of China affected more than mission confidence. According to Harold Isaacs, "The 'loss' of China was part of a larger loss so many Americans suffered at this time, a loss of self-confidence, a loss of assurance about security and power, especially atom-power, a loss of certainty about the shape of the world and America's place in it . . ."[1] But the Communist take-over in China was an important factor in undermining some of the confidence of Christian mis-

sions. Dr. Max Warren wrote of "the haunting anxiety created by
the shock of China."[2] Here had been the church's greatest mission field, where for several decades about one fourth of all
Christian missionary resources were invested.

The fact is that external conditions are no longer altogether
favorable, and these conditions have affected our confidence
about the readiness of the world for the gospel. Our mood of
confidence has been affected also by another development. In
every part of the world there are secularism and materialism.
People appear quite satisfied with this world and its values. Non-
Christian religions have not disappeared but have shown resurgence and missionary zeal. Only one third of the human race has
confessed Jesus Christ as Lord and Saviour. The proportion of
Christians in the world population is not increasing but decreasing. So we have begun to have doubts about how hungry people
are for the gospel. The longing for the true Saviour has not been
the desire given most prominent expression by many of the people of the world. For example, the hunger of the people of the
United States for the gospel is not altogether obvious. One is not
impressed with the hunger for the Good News in the large cities
or small towns of this country. Church membership is large and
impressive, but much of a minister's time is spent not in satis-
fying expressed hunger but in trying to keep a reasonable proportion of church members attending regularly, in maintaining
organization, and in administering a program which, it is hoped,
will attract more people. To be sure, some American Christians
still believe, or want to believe, that whereas materialism and
secularism are widespread in this country, there is still "over
there" somewhere a conscious hunger, a "how long must we
wait?" mood, among primitive peoples. But such a hunger does
not find definite expression to any great degree either in this
country or overseas.

With the experience of world conditions which instead of being favorable now appear to constitute a hindrance to Christian
missions, and with doubt that the world is waiting for the sun-
rise, our confidence in the readiness of the world for the gospel
has been undermined. It must be emphasized that in spite of ap-

pearances there is a readiness for the gospel, that we must recover
confidence and certainty at this point, and that we must have
eyes to see the readiness. Even so, there are some gains in the
present situation. Some of the optimism of previous periods was
rooted in a shallow understanding of the gospel and of the world.
Much of the former optimism was not true to the facts of life or
to the insights of the Scriptures. While the human heart is restless until it rests in the love of God revealed in Jesus Christ, and
therefore is marked by a hunger and a longing, men in every age
have loved darkness rather than light, have been ready to heed
the things of Satan rather than the things of God, and have been
resistant to the Christian faith. There is some gain in the realization of this condition. ". . . we cannot see the real readiness of the
world for Christ unless we are utterly realistic," says Dr. Pierce
Beaver.[3] It is helpful to know just where we stand. There is no
profit in fooling ourselves about the world situation. We no
longer live in a nineteenth-century era when Western powers and
Protestant nations entered new lands and aided, directly or in-
directly, the expansion of the church in those lands; and it is
helpful for the church to admit this.

While we live in an entirely different kind of world, the fact
remains: the world is ready for the Good News. We must recover this very legitimate and significant conviction. It represents a true insight, and it is important for the missionary vision
and commitment of the church. But we cannot accept the same
view of that readiness which was dominant in a former age. The
mood of our day has changed. The kind of readiness described
in promotional addresses and literature of the last century does
not challenge us. But there is a readiness. For us it must suggest
less of an eagerness for the gospel and more of the fact that the
harvest is here and we are here and the world needs the gospel.
How then shall we view it?

First, it is important to recognize that the readiness belongs to
God. The foundation principle is that readiness depends not on
us, or on world conditions, or on human longings, but on God. It
would be difficult to discover in the New Testament a more important or more impressive lesson than this or one more signifi-

cant for missions today. Whether one considers the narrative about Philip and the Ethiopian eunuch (Acts 8) or the story of the Macedonian call (Acts 16), the teaching is clear: God is at work. He prepares the way. He brings the harvest. The "fullness of time" is in His hands. He is not bound. Historical developments do not control Him; He controls them. Because of these facts there are always new opportunities and new possibilities. In the words of Bishop Lesslie Newbigin, "While Christians speak of the closing of doors, new ones are opened which they do not notice. While it is true that in some places men seem to be deaf to the message of the Gospel, in others there is an openly acknowledged hunger and—precisely among many non-Christians —a readiness to acknowledge the incomparable splendour of Jesus Christ."[4]

God is the ruler of the world and the director of the Christian mission, and therefore there is a readiness which never departs, even though often unrecognized. Dr. D. T. Niles speaks of ". . . God's free initiative, the previousness of Jesus Christ in every situation, the all-encompassing work of the Holy Spirit . . ."[5] Because of God's work we meet readiness where we least expect it, are least prepared for it, and where our efforts do not at all deserve it. Many of us have had the experience described by a nurse in India who labored in an obscure primitive village. "It was just as if Christ had prepared it all and was waiting for us."[6] We sow the seed and by God's grace it falls on good ground. We render our witness and service to an individual or group and know that God has been at work there before us. Our mission is made possible by the comprehensive work of the Spirit. No one should realize this more than those engaged in missionary administration. We often witness "the spontaneous expansion of Christianity." We see a harvest which is not due to our efforts and which frequently takes place in spite of them.

Because readiness belongs to God, external appearances and human judgments are not final. A well-to-do cultured gentleman is gracious and courteous. He is generous and kind. His friendliness is impressive. He gives aid to the church and is favorably disposed to religion. To us he appears "ready." Yet security in his possessions and a confidence in his ability to look after himself make him resist the gospel. Far less "ready" in human eyes is the drunkard who denounces religion and rebels against all attempts to help him. But in him is a heart that God has prepared. This man is ready, without knowing it. For all his appearances, he is a field white unto the harvest. We must have the eyes to see this field—any field—and the readiness to harvest it. For we cannot judge from external appearances where God has been at work preparing for the harvest.

If readiness is God's work, it is essential that we be sensitive to and responsive to the leading of His Spirit. We usually think of individual sensitivity and response. Dr. Pierce Beaver expressed it this way: "The messengers will find a response if they are obedient to the illumination and guidance of the Holy Spirit, if they can find the paths opened by that Spirit, if they use all their talents in God's service, if they are without spiritual pride, if they can humbly identify themselves with their hearers and in a two-way conversation communicate with them, learning from them as well as instructing, and bringing a Power into their lives rather than just speaking words."[7]

The importance of this personal obedience to the leading of God's Spirit must be emphasized continually. It is also important that churches and councils of churches and mission agencies be sensitive to the leading of the Spirit. Those charged with the responsibility of administration and leadership in Christian missions must be alert to what the Spirit is saying to the churches. The churches' expeditions into the non-Christian world sometimes depend on decisions of mission boards located far away. The determining of priorities and the openness to new opportunities and strategic frontiers frequently depend on their alertness to open doors, their vision of new possibilities, and their willingness to furnish leadership for new forms and dimensions of missions. "Let us therefore find out the things which in each place we can do together now; and faithfully do them, praying and working always for that fuller unity which Christ wills for his Church,"[8] the New Delhi Assembly urged. One of the greatest needs is for sensitivity at this point, to consider what can be done and should be done by all the churches working together. Such a step calls for collective planning and joint action. There is need for new exploration, new experiments, and new determination in approaching the total mission in a given area with the total resources of the church. This will depend on more than consultation. It depends also on the willingness of churches and agencies to commit their resources—not just their advice—to an approach which seeks more than the gaining of denominational dividends.

In the second place, readiness must be discovered in places and conditions where we often least expect it. The words of the Apostle Paul are suggestive: "A great door and effectual is opened unto me, and there are many adversaries" (1 Corinthians 16:9, K.J.V.). There is often a readiness in places and conditions we consider most discouraging. It may not be comforting to be forced to find our opportunities amidst obstacles and adversaries. But an appraisal, in faith, of the present world scene suggests that precisely in such a situation there are great open doors, and that if we disregard such opportunities we may surrender the hope of world evangelization in our time. Bishop Stephen Neill wrote, "If we no longer have the power to convert communists, then we might well be advised as Christians and Churches just to make our wills and give up the struggle."[9] Likewise, if we no longer have the power to see effectual doors in the midst of unfavorable conditions we may well be advised to give up the struggle. But such defeatism is far removed from that confident spirit of first-century Christianity which prospered in Caesar's household, which did not flee before the might of Rome, which did not surrender in the face of persecution whether petty or severe, and which was not discouraged amidst prevailing mystery religions.

It is encouraging to note that the great days of "the expansion of Christianity" have not been those times when conditions were favorable and the road was easy and the people were "ready." The Book of Acts offers strong testimony to this fact. When we read this account of early Christian missions we can point out the advantage which came from the dispersal of the Jews, the benefits of Roman justice and Roman roads, and unity in language. But unfavorable conditions were just as numerous if not more so.

And we surely do not receive the impression that the Christian faith prospered because the "heathen" were waiting at the city gates with a longing for the Apostle Paul, and that all of the forces in the society of that time gave aid to his missionary work. The furtherance of the gospel in the first century was not due primarily to favorable conditions. It was due to the proclamation of the gospel in season and out of season.

This same generalization is true of the first five centuries of Christian history which saw the "first great advance" in the expansion of Christianity. The events of this expansion have been narrated in detail and with perspective by Dr. Kenneth Scott Latourette. He notes that Christianity came into the world at a time that was extraordinarily propitious for the spread of a new religion. Among reasons for the success of Christianity, Dr. Latourette notes its organization, its inclusiveness, its combinations of intolerance and adaptability, its miracles, and its moral qualities. In addition, the Christian faith "supplied what the Græco-Roman world was asking of religion and philosophy, and did it better than any of its competitors." The emphasis of Dr. Latourette is not on favorable conditions but on the power of the gospel and the faith of its adherents. ". . . at the very beginning of Christianity there must have occurred a vast release of energy, unequalled in the history of the race. . . . Something happened to the men who associated with Jesus."[10]

Throughout the history of the church the great days of expansion have been marked by opposition and adversity. Those were great days because of the determination that the world, ready or not, must be evangelized. The missionary work of Patrick and Columba and Ansgar and Boniface succeeded where there were many adversaries. Ramon Lull and Francis of Assisi did not meet "readiness" but stones from the Muslims. The dynamic ministry of William Carey in India, Adoniram Judson in Burma, and Hudson Taylor in China was carried on in the face of persistent opposition and continuing troubles. The proclamation of the gospel and the establishment of the Christian fellowship among the Auca Indians in Ecuador, the evangelization of Cannibal Valley in western New Guinea, the progress of the gospel among the tribes of eastern Taiwan, have taken place in spite of numerous and various obstacles. In other areas, such as the great new metropolitan centers of Africa and Asia, the gains have been made in the face of indifference and resistance. Many of the most glorious chapters of Christian history have been due to the discovery of the open doors where there was much adversity.

This can be true for us and for our time. Consider two possibilities discussed by Dr. Pierce Beaver. The nationalistic revolutions of our time are taking place all over the world. They have been an important factor in the gaining of independence for more than seven hundred million people since World War II. But in them there have been manifestations of evil as well as good. There have been selfish interests as well as noble aspirations. Some of them have been destructive and disruptive of missionary outreach. Often they have been marked by anti-white and anti-Western demonstrations which have caused serious difficulties for missionary work in a land.

But amidst these revolutions there are many open doors. Barbara Ward, in her book *The Rich Nations and the Poor Nations,* wrote: "Every one of the revolutions we have discussed goes beyond our material concerns and offers a challenge to the quality of our mind and spirit." In these revolutions she notes "the passionate desire for men to see themselves as the equals of other human beings without distinctions of class or sex or race or nationhood . . ." We have the opportunity of offering "the profound root of equality" which is found in the Christian faith with its teaching that "souls are equal before God and that, therefore, their equality is innate, metaphysical, and independent of the vanities of class, race, or culture." We can proclaim that the gospel holds out to them the possibility of a properly human dignity by recognizing them as people who have value in God's sight. Opportunities will remain also after the revolutions have succeeded. "Now that they [the new nations] are running their own affairs, all the grim problems of life face them in the raw: their bounding birth-rates, lack of capital, their desperate poverty, and, above all, the rising expectations of their own people. Every leader who has led his nation to the overthrow of Western influence or colonial rule is now faced with the stark problem: 'What next?' "[11] Here, then, are open doors for the Christian mission, provided the church will take seriously its responsibility in all areas of life.

Resurging non-Christian religions suggest another illustration of finding readiness amidst adversities. Some of these non-Christian religions are, in certain areas, making greater missionary advance and showing greater zeal than is the Christian Church. We are now living in the era of world religions, perhaps not primarily due to the progress of the non-Christian systems but to the fact that transportation and mass communication have brought all people closer together into "one world." At times we have exaggerated the gains of Hinduism, or Muhammedanism, and some forms of Buddhism, but there is no doubt that there is a real resurgence. It is not suggested that Christians find comfort in the gains of rival faiths, but neither is the reaction of fear the proper Christian response. Religious revival is evidence of a search and of a longing for security and meaning for everyday existence. Such hunger provides the Christian Church with the opportunity to communicate a message about the profound root of meaning and security. We also have an opportunity in the longing of so many people today for a world faith that will unite all mankind. These opportunities are increased because of modern transportation and because there is more communication between all peoples of the world. Thousands of adherents of these non-Christian religions are studying in colleges and universities in the United States. Thousands of American Christian students, government workers, and businessmen have daily contact with adherents of these religions.

There is no question but that there are developments today which are discouraging. But the church, if it has eyes to see, will discover some open doors in these same developments and will find a readiness in places and conditions where ordinarily we would least expect it. The church that is alert to open doors in the midst of adversaries will not be lacking in challenging missionary opportunities.

In the third place, there is readiness wherever there is human need. Wherever need exists—hunger, estrangement, fear, ill health, ignorance—there the Christian and the church will find that "the fullness of time" has come. The New Testament makes clear that what is important is not a set of favorable circumstances or an expressed desire for our services but our brother's need. The Good Samaritan responded not to favorable circumstances nor, so far as we know, to an appeal for aid but to his neighbor's predicament. The need of the world may not be greater in our time, but those who are able to respond to need have less excuse than ever before for ignorance of tragic conditions. The fact of the matter is that we are not ignorant. Through mass communication we quickly learn of emergencies everywhere, and we have sufficient knowledge of long-standing conditions of suffering. We have been made aware of the refugee life of thousands of people who are unsettled amidst contemporary revolutions, of the plight of those who live in the area of war in southeast Asia, of discrimination experienced by colored peoples in many parts of the world. We know that hunger is the daily experience of a large proportion of the world's people, that they do not have adequate medical care or educational opportunity. It is unthinkable that Christian people would have any doubt whatsoever, in the face of such conditions, of their opportunity and obligation in these times.

The need is not only for bread and medicine and education. There is also a different kind of need. As a matter of fact, it is the basic one. It is one which can be satisfied only in Jesus Christ. It is because of his need for Jesus Christ that man is ready. Because there is no exception to that need in the whole wide world, there is readiness everywhere. Everywhere the fields are white unto the harvest; everywhere there is fullness of time. If man is lost, then there is readiness whether the terrain is good or bad, whether conditions are favorable or unfavorable, whether the lost person is longing for a search party or not. Basically, therefore, the question of readiness is a question of the faith of the church. Do we believe that man without Jesus Christ is lost? Do we believe that man desperately needs salvation which is available only in Jesus Christ? Do we believe that there is none other name? If we believe these things we must believe also that the world is ready and we must respond in missionary obedience.

To meet the need of the human heart the Christian must be "profoundly available." It is not primarily a matter of going to someone, or of doing something for someone, but of being "present with" that person, of caring enough to stay close. In such a way the love of Christ is communicated. It is that personal communication of His love—through the servant life, through service rendered in His spirit, through genuine identification and involvement, through love that will not let go in spite of sin and failure and rebellion and ingratitude—which will feed the hungry heart.

In the fourth place, we must discover readiness through alertness to new possibilities. Often we fail to see the readiness of the world for the gospel because we think only in terms of traditional methods and patterns. We are too often extremely conservative in our approach to new things. We do not take readily to the use of the new means of proclaiming the gospel which have great promise. Consider the matter of mass communications. Christian missions make a limited use of radio, for example. Governments have been far more alert to recognize and use the potential of radio broadcasting and to give it the priority it deserves. The rapidly increasing number of radio receivers and of transistor radios has produced an increasing opportunity for broadcasts of the Christian message. There is also great opportunity afforded today by transportation which makes it possible to disperse over the world a large number of Christian laymen for witness through secular vocations. We have not used this opportunity in terms of its potential for world evangelization. But mass communications and transportation are but an illustration of the potential for the Christian mission in the church's willingness to change, to respond promptly to new developments of promise, to use the means and methods which will enable us to accomplish our task more effectively.

We have discussed the readiness of the world for the gospel. The readiness is not found in favorable circumstances or in the plea, "How long, how long must we wait?" But there is a readiness today. There appears to be more readiness in the world for the gospel than readiness in the church to respond. The "fullness of time" is here. In the words of Dr. Pierce Beaver, "This is the most exciting time in the Christian mission since our Lord's advent, and the world was never more ready for His coming."[12]

II

The Readiness of the Church
for Christian Missions

Fields are white unto the harvest and the world is ready for the gospel. But is the church ready for the task? This is our question. We begin with attention to the final word in the title of this chapter. You will notice that the word is "missions," not mission. This will be surprising to many people. We hear much today about mission; we hear increasingly little about missions. A familiar slogan in our present-day ecclesiastical jargon is "the mission of the church." Current emphasis is more and more "from missions to mission."

All that the church is and does is mission. The church is mission; that is, it has been sent, and it has a mission. The mission of the church is to express Christ's concern and action for the whole world. In the words of Johannes Blauw, the mission of the church is the actualization of the dominion of Christ in the world. This represents the total purpose and the total program of the church. It is the dimension of the church's whole life and work.

But there is danger, as Bishop Stephen Neill suggests, that if everything is mission, nothing is mission. We can talk about the total mission of the church but become vague about specific thrusts within that total mission. If everything the church does is classed as mission—and it should be—we will need another word for the church's responsibility, as a part of that total mission, for the "heathen" at home and abroad. The word "missions" is used for this responsibility. Missions are concerned with "pressing forward into the world of 'the heathen,'" as Stephen Neill has said.[1] Missions are specific missionary, or evangelistic, expeditions across the frontier of faith and no faith. Such expeditions are an important part of the total mission of the church: the actualization of the dominion of Christ in our world.

Our concern at this time is to consider: How ready is the church for Christian missions? The answer perhaps depends on the meaning we give to the word "ready." We are not asking whether the church gives intellectual assent to the idea of missions. The question is: How willing is the church for missions, how determined to put to work its mental consent, how eager, how intent, for the task? The Apostle Paul said, "I am ready to preach the gospel to you that are at Rome also" (Romans 1:15, k.j.v.). How ready is the church for missions? As a matter of fact, the burden of this chapter is that we are not ready, not intent, not eager, not willing. But the purpose is not to prove a point. The purpose is to stimulate thought, to suggest that readiness for missions involves more than a generalized and vague evangelistic interest, to maintain that missions require the preservation of a specific missionary intent and structure in the church.

It is important that we view this lack of readiness for missions in proper perspective. Much can be said for the health and vitality of Christian missions today. Church members repeat the refrain that the "era of missions" is over, and they easily move on to the assumption that the need and place of missions have passed. Such claims are too infrequently challenged by Christians who should know better. Far too many Christians have succumbed to the practice of acquiescing in every unjust criticism of Christian missions.

The fact of the matter is that missions are not nearly so bad off as some would suggest. The number of professional missionaries is far greater than ever before. The missionary corps is increasingly international. Younger churches have joined older churches in sending out missionaries. There are now Christian missionaries from the East as well as from the West. No longer is the missionary force almost totally Western, almost totally white, and largely Anglo-Saxon. And no longer is the missionary force almost totally professional, for Christian men and women are increasingly responding to the opportunity to witness in secular vocations.

There are other signs of vitality. The missionary home base is now world-wide. The church exists in every land, and therefore there is a much better deployment of Christian forces. A world-wide church now exists. This world-wide church shows remarkable vigor in many ways. Many parts of the church have shared in and contributed to the fresh insights gained from Biblical and theological studies. World Christians now see the missionary task as involving six continents, not only three—Asia, Africa, and Latin America. We have experienced new dimensions of ecumenical progress, which relate mission to unity and unity to mission. The World Council of Churches and the International Missionary Council, each of which represented significant steps in ecumenical advance, have now united. This has brought missionary concern into the heart of the World Council of Churches, to permeate its whole life, and has permeated missionary interest with church concern. The concern for church and for missions is producing an increasing commitment to "joint action for mission," a willingness to confront the total need and opportunity in a given area with the total resources of the whole church. Such an approach replaces the traditional practice of a denomination's using its resources only for work historically related to that denomination.

We cannot give here a full account of the signs of vitality of Christian missions. In some respects this is unfortunate, for the full story of that vitality is unknown to the majority of church members. Much of the hesitancy and pessimism over Christian missions would be relieved if church members were better informed about new and fruitful experiments in evangelism, such as the Islam in Africa project; about the dynamic regionalism represented in the East Asia Christian Conference; about the research and publications of the Department of Missionary Studies of the World Council of Churches. But enough has been written to indicate that we are not overwhelmed by lethargy and that the church is not lacking in commitment. The truth of the matter is that the church is busy on many important Christian fronts. Christian people show devotion to excellent causes, and they are alert to many new opportunities. They are favorable to

mission and missions. But for all of this there are signs that we
are lacking in Paul's kind of readiness for Christian missions, for
specific missionary expeditions across the frontier of faith and no
faith, and that we are not pressing forward into the world of the
heathen at home and abroad.

The situation is suggested in the words of Bishop Lesslie Newbigin:

> Why is the missionary advance of the Church so slow? Why are
> the missionary forces of the Church apparently so immobile, so
> completely exhausted by the effort to remain where they are? Why
> is it that the missionaries sent out by the churches which belong
> to the World Council of Churches are a decreasing proportion of
> the total missionary force? Why is it, to speak frankly, that the
> very word "missionary" has become a bad word in many Christian
> circles, so that while secular governments and other religions take
> it freely into use, Christians appear to be afraid of it? Why is it
> that among the best and most devoted of young people in our
> churches one hears it said, "Anything, anywhere, as long as it is
> not as a missionary"?[2]

All of this adds up to what can be described as a lack of readiness for missions. There is a reason for this and an answer to
Bishop Newbigin's question, "Why?" These are to be found in
the neglect of specific missionary intent in the life of the church
and the neglect of specific missionary concentration in the structure of the church. This is the thesis of this chapter. If this thesis
can be substantiated, then the reader should be able to draw
some conclusions about the remedy for the situation and about
his own part in that remedy.

Let us look first at the neglect of the specific missionary intent.
This means that the center of our concern has become not the
world but the ecclesiastical world. We spend most of our time
and resources in feeding and nurturing members, with little effort
directed toward the non-Christian. The extension or reconquest
of ecclesiastical influence, the winning back of those alienated
from the church, and the perfecting of the ecclesiastical machinery frequently become our chief interest and goal. Our concern
centers in the dissemination of Christianity and the planting of

churches rather than in the proclamation of the gospel to today's heathen.

This analysis assumes that "planting of churches" is different from the proclamation of the gospel to the heathen, that "church extension" is not the same as Christian missions. It must be emphasized that church extension is one of the most important tasks of the church. The pages of this book will seek to make clear just how important this task is. It is of the greatest significance for Christian missions. Church extension at times leads to missions, and missions are not unrelated to or unconcerned about the planting of churches.

But there is a difference between these two. The difference, small but significant, relates primarily to attitude and focus. This difference has been emphasized by Christian writers from the East and from the West, from younger and from older churches. J. C. Hoekendijk, for example, distinguishes between churchification and evangelization. D. T. Niles sees a difference between maintaining and deepening and broadening a church's life and the expansion of a church's life. The late Dr. Walter Freytag emphasized that missions are never simply the transplanting or extension of a church's life. Missions mean more than what takes place when a church "colonizes." A church is involved in Christian missions not when it is extending itself but when it shows the willingness to fall into the ground and die, becoming thereby a step toward something new. So Dr. Freytag could write: ". . . of the proclamation of the Gospel something new always comes into being."[3] These writers suggest that the primary concern of missions is not the extension of the church as an institution. The focus of missions is the expeditions across the frontier of faith and no faith, while the focus of church extension is the institutional church and its members.

The lack of readiness (eagerness) for missions is related to our focus. We have become ecclesiastically oriented instead of Kingdom-centered; institution-minded instead of proclamation-conscious. All of this is to say that our primary intent has ceased to be missionary expeditions into the world of the heathen and has become instead the transplanting or expansion of churches. This situation can be viewed on the home front—whether the home front be America or Asia. All of us are familiar with home missions and home missionaries. Home missions were in the beginning the thrust of the church into new unreached regions. What are home missions today in the United States? They are for the most part churches in settled if not static communities which are unable to support a "full" program. Few of these churches today are involved in a missionary thrust into the world of the heathen. The home missionary is no longer chiefly engaged in missionary expeditions. Home missions and home missionaries today are chiefly involved in the ecclesiastical domain, more absorbed with the church than with the world, almost totally directed toward the feeding of members rather than an approach to the non-member. Home missions today do not represent, as they once did, an aspect of the church's life dominated by a specific missionary intent. They represent an aspect of the church's life which is dominated by the whole idea of church extension.

This same process, the neglect of specific missionary intent, is under way in the church's overseas work. The missionary intention was preserved for a longer period in "foreign" missions. But here also we are now becoming absorbed in the ecclesiastical world to the neglect of the non-Christian frontier. An increasing proportion of our energies is devoted to the maintenance of churches and institutions for Christians, and to concern for broadening and deepening the life of younger churches rather than in a fresh confrontation with the missionary frontier. All of this has contributed to a loss of mobility, to the problem of institutionalism, and to the "mission station" mind.

This situation is becoming a cause of deep concern for overseas mission agencies. For example, the mission board with which I am related has made a determined effort through the years to remain committed to "pressing forward into the world of the heathen." The purpose of our program has been frequently reaffirmed: "The great end of missionary life and service is the preaching of Christ and Him crucified to the non-evangelized peoples. All forms of missionary work must be subordinate to this end."[4] ". . . the true ends of missionary work are the preaching of the gospel to every creature in order to the salvation of souls and the establishment in each separate nation of an independent, self-sustaining, and self-propagating church."[5] Yet a large, perhaps increasingly large, proportion of our resources is devoted to work among Christian people, for Christian people, in Christian institutions. And a large part of our time is absorbed in consultations with sister churches overseas about proper structures of relationship between churches. This situation exists in spite of the fact that in six of nine fields where we have missionaries the number of Christians, including Roman Catholics and Protestants, amount to less than 8% of the population, and in eight of the nine fields the Protestant believers form less than 5% of the population.

It should be emphasized that work among Christian people, for Christian people, and in Christian institutions is exceedingly important. It is important for Christian missions. Our goal is the evangelization of the world. A great hope for the evangelization of large areas of the world is to be found in the younger church in an area which has become a missionary community. To strengthen a church that it may serve as a cutting edge for missions, to give it interchurch aid so that it can more effectively live and work for the actualization of Christ's dominion, to share with it our missionary passion, is a use of our missionary resources of the highest merit and significance.

There is the danger, however, that interchurch aid for missions will become simply interchurch aid, a support of organizational and institutional life which has ceased to have a missionary cutting edge. It is this danger which Dr. Pierce Beaver has in mind in writing, ". . . the missionary enterprise is in great measure a colossal system of inter-church aid, with relatively little pioneer evangelistic advance."[6] Commenting on these words, Dr. Donald McGavran said: " 'The colossal system of inter-church aid' passes for good missions—whether the younger Churches grow or not. If we are aiding them, that is good mission policy. The 'no-growth' situation is accepted without remorse."[7] It will be seen from these statements that the lack of readiness for missions is true not only of the older churches but also of many of the younger churches. This is not surprising, for conditions in the "sending" churches will be reflected also in the "receiving" churches. And younger churches will contribute their share to a situation of immobility. Dr. J. C. Hoekendijk reminds us, "It is sad but true that even in the younger churches the second generation of Christians becomes established and immobile. And for a next generation, Christian life has often already become an unexciting business of routine."[8]

All of this, it is suggested, is due to the neglect of the specific missionary intent in the life of the church. When we fail to preserve and nurture the determination for missionary expeditions across the frontier of faith and no faith, we experience at home and abroad ". . . this inveterate tendency of the Church to localize, to stabilize, and to organize . . ."[9]

We have been occupied in these pages with the lack of readiness for missions. This lack, so our thesis affirms, is due to the neglect of the specific missionary intent. It is also related to the neglect of specific missionary concentration in the structure of the church. The failure of missionary purpose inevitably has its effect. A major effect is the loss in the organized church structure of an adequate focus of deliberate concentration for pressing forward into the world of the heathen. This is to say that a church that no longer has a specific missionary purpose will no longer create or preserve in its structure an agency solely and specifically devoted to implementing missions. When the missionary intent is strong, the church insists on the structure to implement it. With the weakening of this intention there is less concern that there be in the organized church an agency which concentrates exclusively on efforts directed toward the non-Christian. The weakening of this structure for missionary outreach in turn further weakens the intention for missions. Soon readiness for missions is no longer reflected in the church's literature, or budget, or promotion, or structure.

We may again look at developments at home and abroad which support this part of our thesis. In the early days of our country, home mission committees and home mission boards served as the point of concentration for missions at home. Their job was missions. Now, while home mission committees and home mission boards exist, they no longer, for the most part, represent a structure specifically and exclusively dedicated to pressing forward into the world of the heathen. They now have a multitude of duties, including church extension, and one of the least of these duties, it appears, is the leadership of the church in expeditions across the frontier of faith and no faith.

An illustration can be found in the Board of Church Extension of one denomination. In this Board there is a Division of Home Missions, with six departments. The Missionary Support Department has three emphases: "progress toward self-support," "adequate salaries for home mission workers," "the organization of new churches in all areas of promise." The Survey and Church Location Department has as its main function "the rendering of assistance to presbytery church extension committees and local groups in the wisest possible location of churches." The Church Architecture Department shares an important function, but it is not specifically directed to pressing forward into the world of the heathen. The Town and Country Church Department gives major emphasis to "improving both the program and the leadership of the rural churches of our Assembly." The Chaplains and Military Personnel Department does not list specific concern for missions. Until recently there was a Negro Work Department: "Through visits for counseling and establishment of workshops we are endeavoring to strengthen Negro churches to do a better job for their people."

In the Board of Church Extension there is also a Division of Evangelism. Here is a point of concentration for missions. But a considerable portion of the energies of this Division is directed to helping churches in the "care of new members," the care of "members that move," and the "renewal and reorientation of inactive members."

This Board of Church Extension has important functions which are effectively discharged and which make a significant contribution to the life and work of the church. The emphasis I am trying to make is that if there is any point of concentration in the structure of the church for missions at home, it is here. But this focal point of concentration for missions has become dulled. Home missions and evangelism, once independent agencies, are now subordinated in a board of church extension. They have become burdened with many duties not specifically related to missions. There remains no agency in this denomination whose primary responsibility is to lead and encourage the church to make missionary expeditions at home. In the structure of the church there is no longer a specific concentration for the home missionary task.

Experience in overseas work is similar. A church sets up a board of missions to serve as the point of concentration for foreign missionary endeavor. In this way the church organizes for this work and makes provision in its structure for the concentration necessary to accomplish the task. But the situation gradually changes. The agency becomes busy with a multitude of assignments. An increasing amount of its energy is required, it appears, for promotion at home. More and more missionary speakers and conferences and an increasing amount of missionary literature— all directed at church people—are needed to keep the home church informed about the overseas activities and interested in continuing and increasing support.

In the foreign field the board becomes increasingly involved in providing services which, it is hoped, foster a missionary spirit in a sister church and which strengthen that church for missions. For example, it devotes a considerable amount of its funds and personnel to service in Christian institutions. These institutions are exceedingly important. They train many who press forward into the world of the heathen. They can be instruments for a missionary thrust into a particular segment of non-Christian society. Many have a missionary cutting edge. But they can lose that cutting edge and become immobile institutions. In any case, the personnel of a mission agency can work less and less with non-Christians and become increasingly involved in training others who will work with non-Christians. Further, the administration of a large number of institutions can absorb the board in important concerns which detract from its concentration on the main task of missions.

Almost inevitably this will prove to be the case. A small beginning in primary education leads to secondary education and colleges, so that soon the mission board serves as a board of Christian higher education. Sending personnel to university campuses for a pioneering missionary ministry among students leads the mission board to involvement in a world-wide campus Christian life program, with many administrative decisions required. Similarly the mission board becomes involved in a program for the men of the church, for the women of the church. All of these are important services. But they lead the mission agency to involvement in deepening and broadening of the church's life and in administration, to the neglect of serving primarily as the point of concentration for overseas expeditions into the world of the heathen.

It is doubtful whether a foreign mission board can remain the point of concentration for missions if it carries all of these duties. One direction which deserves more study is the possibility of the mission board's surrendering its administration of colleges to the denomination's agency which carries that responsibility for colleges at home, and its campus Christian life program and its program for men and women to those agencies of the denomination which exist for these purposes. Many questions can be raised about this approach. A major objection is that the mission agency and the home church would feel that with all of these activities turned over to other agencies, hardly a sufficient responsibility will be left for the mission board. But the most valuable function which the mission board can render is not maintaining and administering a multitude of important programs. The greatest service it can render to the church and for the Kingdom of God is just this: to serve solely as a point of concentration in that church's structure for efforts to proclaim the gospel to the two billion people who do not accept Jesus Christ as Lord and Saviour. Such a point of concentration is so important that the church should insist on it. Provisions should be made by the church for interchurch aid, of course. But it should preserve in its structure an agency whose chief responsibility is to inspire and channel the resources of the church so that those resources can be

brought to bear on the missionary task. No church which allows
the loss of a specific missionary concentration in the structure of
the church will long maintain its missionary thrust.

Of course, a point of concentration for missions is necessary at
all levels of the church's life. This is not something that can be
left with church courts, up the ecclesiastical ladder. There must
be, in the words of a current emphasis, "the missionary structure
of the congregation." This emphasis does not refer to the organization of a missions committee in a congregation but to the shape
of the congregation's total life and organization. The shape of the
congregation's life, its structure, will seriously affect its ability to
be an effective missionary community. But while the total life
and organization of the congregation must be missionary, it will
be surprising if there will not be needed a specific group or
agency in the congregation which is given responsibility for leading the congregation in missionary outreach and in alertness to
the missionary situation of the congregation. The congregation
will also need a structure which will ensure its continuing involvement in missions to the end of the earth. No congregation
will preserve a readiness for missions if its involvement in missions
overseas is only in terms of a mission board's program. A congregation's involvement in "foreign" missions should be a direct
participation in expeditions into the non-Christian world, not
simply using its resources to make it possible for others of that
denomination to go on such expeditions, and not simply to support a "board" program.

Our thesis has been that we are lacking in readiness for missions, due to a neglect of missionary intent in the life of the
church and of missionary concentration in the structure of the
church. One cannot easily estimate all the evils of such a course.
In the words of Dr. Egbert W. Smith, "No institution can repu-
diate its fundamental purpose, its main reason for being, and not
suffer."[10] Christian history provides examples of the church in
other periods experiencing the results of neglecting missions,
even if in other respects it had much of which to boast. Dr. Eugene L. Smith comments on the church in the seventh century
which was overwhelmed by Muhammedanism.

The defeats of the seventh century came to a church large in numbers, dominant in politics, powerful in leadership, rich in money, history, and intellect. The defeats came not alone because of outward threat, but in part because of inner spiritual weakness. That weakness was the failure of a great church to keep alive its sense of witness, to maintain a constant outreach in love, in the name of Jesus Christ, to its neighbors both near and far.[11]

The neglect of missions, according to Bishop Newbigin, affects the fundamental forms of the church's life. "The ministry is conceived almost exclusively in pastoral terms as the care of souls already Christian. The congregation is seen as a body existing for the edification and sanctification of its own members rather than for witness and service to the world outside. Our very systems of doctrine tend to be constructed *vis-à-vis* other Christian systems, rather than *vis-à-vis* the great non-Christian systems of thought. And the normal content of a course in Church history has far more of the mutual disputes of Christians than of the missionary advances of the Church and the encounter of the gospel with the non-Christian cultures which it has successively met and mastered."[12] We become, as Dr. John Mackay reminds us, more concerned for the proprieties of ecclesiastical order than for the demands of missionary ardor. A "narcissitic" preoccupation with itself begins to influence the church, contributing to a low level of boredom in many members and ministers. In short, the results of neglect of missionary intention and concentration are such as described by Dr. J. C. Hoekendijk: "We have run aground. . . . We have become second-rate descendants in the Christian mission. . . . Consequently our evangelism at present consists almost exclusively of superficial missions, of ecclesiastical coastal navigation, of spiritual suburban traffic. . . ."[13]

Such conditions need not continue. But the remedy must be in terms of the problem. Devotion to pressing forward into the world of the heathen will not spring from a generalized mission interest. Far more will be required. Readiness for Christian missions requires a firm conviction about the gospel. We will not be ready, intent, eager to proclaim the gospel if we are not sure about it, if we are not certain that Jesus Christ is the only Saviour, if we are not convinced that man is lost without the gospel. Readiness for missions is related to the fundamental themes of the Christian faith. The recovery of specific missionary purpose will result only from a renewal of the church's life through prayer and Bible study which are more than exercises. And that missionary intent will have to be preserved and expressed, even protected, by provision for specific missionary concentration in the structure of the church; that is, insisting on an agency which has the responsibility of leading the church in expeditions into the world of the heathen. There must be that discipline in the life and program and structure of the church which insists, "This one thing I do." The recovery of the readiness for missions demands costly sacrifice.

The cost, however great, will be justified. When mission and missions become real, members and ministers will reflect the change. Nothing but boredom can be expected when the major concern is the recovery of lost ecclesiastical ground, or winning back alienated members, or self-centered service of an institution. But to become obedient servants of the proclamation of the gospel across the frontier of faith and no faith will give us a sense of mission which is of the essence of life itself. In the words of Bishop Newbigin:

> . . . That sense of awe and wonder in the presence of Jesus belongs, if I may dare to put it so, at the growing edge of the Church, at the point where Christ is actually subduing men to himself, at the point where men are learning for the first time who he is, at the point, therefore, where they cannot keep silent. Concern about that growing edge is at the same time concern for the life of the Church itself, for that hidden life of communion and adoration without which the Church cannot live, and out of which alone can spring a true, loving, humble, and inexhaustible missionary passion.[14]

For "Where His word is preached and heard, where consciences are first rebuked and then consoled, where the proud are humbled and the despairing lifted up, where the parched ground of dead hearts is changed by the quickening Spirit into a garden yielding fruit to the glory of God, there the Church celebrates the triumph of its Lord; there by faith it triumphs with Him."[15]

III

Theology of Missions: Escape or Encounter?

It is not surprising that concern for the growing edge of the church leads to consideration of theological matters. Christian missions are the fruit of sound Christian theology. They must rest on Biblical and theological foundations and be the product of the church's continuing and fresh reflection on the meaning of the gospel. It is that continuing and fresh reflection on the gospel which creates and strengthens the missionary intent. The development of a theology of missions is the attempt to bring our view of Christian missions, and therefore our conduct of them, into harmony with the fundamental themes of Scripture. It is an attempt to answer such questions as: What are Christian missions, why do we engage in them, and what is their purpose? But it should also be an attempt to answer questions about our own missionary purpose and actions.

The importance of a theology of missions is suggested in the words of Dr. W. A. Visser 't Hooft about a theology of the ecumenical movement.

> We need such a theology of the ecumenical movement because a Christian movement without theology is like a ship without a rudder. The choices which must be made, the decisions which have to be taken imply assumptions about the task of the ecumenical movement. . . . And if one acts without any realization that theological issues are involved, one is likely to follow non-theological principles which are only a nice expression for worldly motives.
>
> We also need a theology for the ecumenical movement in order to arrive at clear common criteria by which we can evaluate its work, its utterances. . . . Now it is impossible to arrive at clear

criteria unless we work out a coherent conception of the total task of the ecumenical movement, and we cannot see that task as a whole until we succeed in answering the basic questions about its raison d'être and about the implications which its existence has for the life of the churches.[1]

It must not be assumed that theology of missions concerns only "higher" echelons of the church. Whether recognized or not, this matter is before every congregation. Each local fellowship of believers is making decisions on assumptions about the nature of its task. It needs a theology to establish criteria by which it evaluates its life and work. Further, each congregation will increasingly face questions about the missionary motive and obligation and about the justification for presenting the claims of Christ to persons of other religious allegiance. Men and women of other faiths are in our universities and communities. Sometimes they are brought to our churches and into our homes. We live more and more in a society of religious pluralism. The time is long past when the "heathen" are far away, when it could be assumed that all of them are ignorant and poor. They are in our society now, and many are seen to be competent and attractive people. Some of them reveal depths of integrity and discipline and poise. Some of them become known to Christians in a personal way, and bonds of friendship are established. Christians and congregations will face as never before the question whether we deeply believe that there is salvation in none other name than that of Jesus Christ.

If a theology of missions is vital for congregations, it is also essential for the church's missionary operation. In this realm also there is need for basic assumptions concerning the nature of the task and for clear criteria by which missions can be evaluated. The extent of this need is indicated in the following appraisal of the missionary outreach of one denomination:

. . . American Lutherans have not formulated "clear theological principles on which our pursuit of world missions is based." . . . We have no theological interpretation of the non-Christian religions . . . and no clear theological treatments of our purpose. So we have had to muddle through. . . . Our promotional material is designed merely to keep the wheels going and, often, is propa-

gandistic. . . . We have a monopoly on financial and organizational policies and know-how, but no understanding of the missionary task as related to theology.[2]

The need for and the importance of a missions theology have
stimulated study and action. Theological alertness and missionary
concern have been manifested in the abundant efforts of recent
years to arrive at an adequate theology of missions. Many of the
most fruitful efforts have been results of ecumenical ventures.
Christians from all over the world, "mutually encouraged by
each other's faith," have shared their knowledge and insights
gained in their search for a Biblical view of the missionary
enterprise of the church. Various Christian traditions and
churches have contributed to this effort. The period since 1951
has been very fruitful. For in preparation for the Willengen
Conference of the International Missionary Council in 1951 there
was world-wide study of the Biblical and theological foundations
of Christian missions. The study was prompted by the realization
that the most crucial matter for Christian missions was not the
state of the international situation but the church's view of missionary obligation. The results of the conference were published
in the volume, *The Missionary Obligation of the Church*. An
understanding of the place of the Willengen discussions in terms
of developments before and since 1951 will be possible through
the study of Wilhelm Andersen's little book, *Towards a Theology
of Mission*. It is possible also in that little book to sense something
of the important issues which are at stake.

Since Willengen, theology of missions has received continuing
attention. The church has been active on this front. Some of the
best Christian minds and hearts have been at work. Much of the
leadership was furnished by the International Missionary Council, now a part of the World Council of Churches. The Department of Missionary Studies of the Division of World Mission and
Evangelism of the World Council has been busy for several years
on this subject. Out of a study on "The Word of God and the
Church's Missionary Obedience," has come the book by Johannes
Blauw, *The Missionary Nature of the Church*, and D. T. Niles's
book, *Upon the Earth*. Out of this same context has also come the

World Council pamphlet, *The Missionary Task of the Church—
Theological Reflections*. Also from World Council circles has
come a study pamphlet by Lesslie Newbigin, *Trinitarian Faith
and Today's Mission*. This is not an effort toward a theology of
missions but a stimulating essay which demonstrates the practical
relevance of theological matters. Bishop Newbigin shows the
resources and guidance for today's mission which are to be found
within "the framework of a fully and explicitly trinitarian doctrine of God."[3] The doctrine of the Trinity points the way, he
finds, for the solution of three perplexing problems in the present
missionary situation. The above writings have been mentioned as
examples of the vitality of the church in the important task of
arriving at a Biblical view of missions. One other writing, Gerald
H. Anderson's *The Theology of the Christian Mission*, will provide a "feel" for the variety of viewpoints and the nature of the
issues in the current discussions.

It is not only in ecumenical circles, however, that theology of
missions has received attention. Many churches of Christendom
have recognized their involvement in this matter and its importance for them. The following brief review indicates the experience of one American church, the Presbyterian Church in the
United States.

In this church, theology of missions has received frequent
attention in the official actions of the church as well as in unof-
ficial discussions and studies. In 1952 the General Assembly of
this church appointed, in response to an overture, an Ad Interim
Committee to study the church's overseas mission work, including
the theological basis. This committee worked for two years, making its report in 1954. During the following year the Board of
World Missions studied the report and formulated its own answer
and brought the matter to the attention of the General Assembly.
In 1959 the matter was again introduced. World Mission chairmen from all over the church requested a statement of the
Board's theology of missions. The World Mission chairmen
stated: "There is a need for the theological basis of our World
Mission enterprise to be more clearly articulated. The root of any
endeavor of the Church is theological, and when this is forgotten

there is a drift toward conclusions which cannot withstand careful examination or inspire real commitment. We need to hear clearly stated the theology upon which rests our understanding of the missionary motive. Are souls eternally damned if we fail to carry the message of Christ to them or can we leave this question to God and still have a valid Christian imperative?"[4] The Board of World Missions took this request seriously and published a pamphlet, "Some Theological Bases of World Missions."

Still again in 1959 a presbytery overtured the General Assembly to appoint an Ad Interim Committee to study "the whole philosophy of World Missions." This overture was the primary factor which led to the well-known Consultation on World Missions at Montreat, North Carolina, October 1962. The Consultation Recommendations included a strong theological statement which was approved and given wide distribution by the Board of World Missions.[5] The recommendations also contained a request that "The publication program of the Board include an increased emphasis on the theological basis of our mission."[6] Within a month of the Consultation one of the church's seminaries asked for a statement of the Board's theology of missions, with a request for an explanation and justification of that theology. Again within a few weeks it was recommended that "the Board of World Missions sponsor a special study of the theology of missions, and report the results to the Church." Throughout this period, theology of missions has been before the church constantly. It does not appear, however, that results have been very fruitful or that all questions and issues have been answered satisfactorily. Consider some aspects of this church's experience.

All of the requests were directed at "foreign mission" circles. The demands were legitimate and important demands. Basically they were asking, "Do you know what you are doing?" There was desire that the programs we were pursuing overseas should not contradict the nature of the task to be performed. Christian missions are not to be conducted as ecclesiastical extension, or as propaganda, or as a crusade to be brought to victory by individual effort, but as obedient participation in God's plan for the world. The demands for missions theology were asking that in missions we be alert. There are new and helpful insights, and new and fresh statements of fundamental Christian doctrines. We are living in a creative period of vital Biblical and theological study. The church has every right to expect that those who oversee the missionary outreach of the church are familiar with these studies and bring to bear on the church's mission the sound insights of the best scholarship of our time. The demands for a theology of missions were asking for leadership. On the basis of theological alertness and reflection on the church's nature and task, those who direct the foreign mission work of the church have a responsibility for leadership. Concentration on the missionary task should lead to deeper insights which are shared with the church. A mission agency has responsibility for leadership not only in method and strategy but also in developing within the church a sound Biblical understanding of the nature and mission of the church.

The concern for a theology of missions was not directed to seminaries and theologians but to missionary circles. The explanation may be that there was assumption of lack of theological alertness in mission circles. But there are at least two other explanations. First, the requests were directed to mission circles on the incorrect assumption that theology of missions is a special kind of theology. It is sometimes inferred that theology of missions is separate from the church's theology. To correct this error it has been suggested that we talk not of theology of missions but of missionary theology. Theology of missions is an attempt to keep in perspective the missionary dimensions and implications of all Christian theology. Second, the requests were directed to mission circles because of concern for an honest answer to a special question: Are souls eternally damned if we fail to carry the message of Christ to them or can we leave this question to God and still have a valid Christian imperative? There are indications that the real interest in all the demands for a theology of missions was not missions or theology but the question of whether those who have never heard of Christ are going to hell.

It is interesting to note that during this entire ten-year period there were no overtures calling for a statement of the theological foundation of another part of the church's life. Pastoral counsel-

ing was in its prime, but there were no official requests for the
theology of pastoral counseling. Seminary professors and students
were not asked for a theology of theological education. There
were no overtures demanding that a pastor give a frequent account of the theology of ministry. Christian laymen and departments of laity were not asked to defend their theological understanding of their activities. The Board of Women's Work was not
directed to state a theology of women's work. The request for a
theology of missions was never laid at the door of home mission
circles. It was always directed at "foreign" mission circles. Before
one study of mission theology was completed there was demand
for another. Such a situation may reflect a serious interest in the
subject and may be in part a result of the valuable studies in
ecumenical circles. What appears more probable, and more disturbing, is that "theology of missions" had become a hobby, a
theoretical interest, the best topic for an armchair discussion.
This is said in description of the general situation, not of specific requests or overtures. The interest was in "theology of
missions," not in a vital missionary theology. The actions of the
church do not reveal an urgent desire to know in order to be and
do. The purpose appears to have been to settle points of debate,
not to enter upon expeditions across the frontier of faith and
no faith. During these years there was a declining evangelistic
zeal and a decrease in the visible results of evangelism. When a
statement of theology of missions was completed, it did not become the basis of new commitment and obedience but the occasion for a new study. Although the best literature on mission
theology was given wide distribution, the desire for new theology
was not satisfied. A theology of missions had become the pass-
word for sophisticated theological circles.

It is to the danger of theology of missions as a popular pastime
that we now turn. It must be emphasized again that the serious
attention given to this subject throughout Christendom is absolutely essential and may be a channel of what the Spirit is saying
to the churches. But there is another side of the story. It is this
other side which requires some consideration. There are dangers
in the present situation. In citing the dangers, there can be no
disparagement of the creative and sound labors of theologians

or of the role of genuine theology. We will make no gains whatsoever in anti-intellectualism or in questioning the merit of disciplined thought and study. The fact is, however, that some of the
popular concern with theology of missions appears an academic
and theoretical interest which leads to escape, not to encounter.

In the first place, theoretical interest in missions theology may
lead us to substitute theology of missions for missions. I have in
mind, of course, armchair interest and "speculative" theology.
Dr. Hendrik Kraemer has warned us that, "Our famous good
theology of today is becoming far too much a sort of fondled
treasure about which we are happy." And he adds, "This I re-
gard as a temptation of the devil himself!"[7] While two out of
every three people in the world do not confess Jesus Christ as
Lord and Saviour, while the proportion of Christians in our
world becomes smaller day by day, while the population ex-
plodes, while in some lands young churches exist as tiny minori-
ties in a population that is ninety-nine percent outside of the
Christian fold, we may continue our theological knitting and our
theological hairsplitting, our theologizing, and even convince
ourselves that this is the real thing. At such a time we need to remember the words of O. Michel: "All genuine theology is in
battle against theologizing, abstracting, theorizing, and against
the attempt to replace the genuine Biblical and historical motive
by a philosophical transformation."[8]

The fact is that theory of missions can exist without missions
and thus become a form of religion without decision. Consider
an illustration. An article written by Dr. Kenneth Keniston in
the Phi Beta Kappa publication, *The American Scholar*, discussed today's undergraduates. The author found them "politi-
cally disengaged." They substitute the "trivia" of campus politics
for involvement in "true politics." They remain "restrained,
reflective, cautious, intellectual and even pedantic," with a "lack
of deep commitment to adult values."[9] A Harvard Medical School
psychiatrist has commented on the modern defense mechanisms
which are used to keep from facing the actualities of nuclear war
possibilities. One of these is "intellectualization." He states that
the expert's knowledge of the technical aspects of nuclear war
may serve to keep him somehow quite distant from the psycho-

logical and political realities. These words may be suggestive of a situation among ourselves. It is entirely possible that much of our armchair interest in theological discussion of missions can be a form of "disengagement," a substitution of the "trivia" of mission discussion for involvement in missions, "intellectualization" as a defense mechanism and as an escape mechanism, a theorizing about missionary activity as a substitute for pressing forward into the world of the heathen at home and abroad.

The danger of substituting academic discussion for pressing into the world of the heathen, at home and abroad, may be very real for some who are otherwise among the most progressive and ecumenically minded ministers and members of the church. There are those who assert that they would commit themselves to service overseas as professional missionaries if only the mission agency became theologically alert, if it accepted and implemented an adequate theology of missions. Of course, one mission agency is not the only channel for Christian missions. If a particular mission agency is not a proper channel, is not theologically alert, let the would-be missionary go elsewhere, but let him serve. Inadequacy of a particular channel does not justify the abandonment of a missionary vocation. But there is some evidence that those who state that they would become involved in pressing forward into the world of the heathen overseas if only a sounder theology of missions were developed do not always follow through on this promise.

A year or two ago I was speaking to an official of a sister mission board. He told me that the mission agency he represented had long been concerned about attracting more theologically alert young men and women for service overseas. It wanted candidates who were familiar with the insights of Barth and Brunner and Tillich and Niebuhr and Bultmann. It coveted those who were committed to theological inquiry. It desired those of deep social concern and those who had a deep commitment to the church, not simply to pious individualism. The agency was advised that it could not hope to attract many of this group unless it had an image before the church of alertness and of progress, of openness to new methods, of willingness to rethink, and unless it was theologically alert and up-to-date. It appears that the mission board

understood that if it only would change its ways it would receive
more theologically alert applicants than could be used. The mission agency worked out an up-to-date strategy and took a prominent place in alert missionary leadership. It led in the composi-
tion of one of the most excellent statements of missionary
theology. But all of this did not produce an appreciable increase
in the number of theologically alert young men and women who
volunteered for mission service. The board official said to me
rather forlornly, "In spite of all of this, two-thirds of all of our
missionary candidates still come from the fundamentalist wing of
our Church." This parallels, to some extent, the experience of
the mission agency of many of the old-line denominations. The
fact of the matter is that they receive few applicants from societies of theological inquiry. It would be of great benefit if missionary candidates showed a deeper interest in theology and
theological courses, in theological debate and inquiry. But it
would also help if members of societies of theological inquiry
would commit themselves to a pressing forward into the world
of the heathen at home and abroad.

There would be a rich reward for such volunteers and for the
Christian cause if theologically concerned and theologically
equipped young men and women would commit themselves in
greater numbers not only to mission but to missions. This would
result, for one thing, in a very real contribution to theology of
missions. Such young men and women could contribute to the
theological vitality of the younger churches. They could influence
the theological character of the world church of tomorrow. They
could stimulate a missionary theology in the older and younger
churches and in the world church.

We return now to the suggestion that there is a danger of
substituting theoretical discussion about missions for missions.
Of course, this is tragic for the church. As an example, consider
once again the church of the seventh century, which helped to
usher in a thousand years of uncertainty and was in many areas
overwhelmed by Muhammedanism. The comment of Dr. Eugene
L. Smith on that church is again helpful.

> . . . The church had become, in many respects, a vast debating
> society. It was dominated by men who were hot on the quest of a

perfect theological definition. Moreover, that definition was to be made in the classical languages, not in the tongues of the people. The intellects of the church were thus occupied with the development of formulas rather than with the formulation of effective patterns of Christian witness. The church's thought was turned in upon itself, rather than out upon the world for which Christ died. When this process becomes complete within any church, it has unknowingly signed its own death warrant.[10]

In the second place, theology of missions as a popular pastime may lead us to forget that Christian missions begin with the gospel, not with theology. We do well to remember that missionary obligation roots in the gospel, and to recall the words of Dr. Nels Ferré, that "A theology of missions adds nothing to the Christian faith."[11] This is what we are apt to forget, that theological exercises cannot add one cubit to the stature of the gospel. When theology is not an academic scheme but an exciting process which originates in a careful and attentive reading of the Scriptures, it is of great value. Theological reflection on the great themes of Scripture can aid in our understanding of the Christian faith. But even so, theology can add nothing to the gospel.

One of the mistakes of our modern infatuation with the practical is the belief that another method or a new technique will solve our problem. Theologians—amateur and professional— have warned us of this illusion. But we face a similar danger with respect to theology. We appear to believe that a new theology of missions will get the job done. As a matter of fact, we appear to believe that the newer the theology of missions, the surer the results. Dr. George Sweazey has written, "Those who write and plan for 'evangelism' seem often to be straining for the novel because they are jaded with the old words and old methods . . ." He added, perhaps unfairly, "If you invite a typical young professor of theology to your church for a lectureship, you may find that he is willing to talk about the Gospel of John, but not greatly interested. What he really burns to explain to our baffled members is the crypto-Christianity in Kafka, or the hidden gospel themes in Henry Miller."[12] There are parallels in missionary circles. It is time that we recognize that theology, even new theology, is not the primary thing. Dr. Hendrik Kraemer has some

sobering words for us: "We are under the delusion that the so-
called problem of evangelism can mainly be solved by the direct
way either of good theology or of good and new methods or of
very well planned actions. . . . Let me add . . . that under 'good
theology' I mean also the important matter of what is called 'new
ways of communication' and a 'new language for translating the
Christian message . . .' "[13]

What is basic is not theology but the gospel. All of our deep
interest in the theology of missions must not lead to the forget-
fulness of this fact. After all, it is the gospel that is productive.
Russell T. Hitt records in his book, *Cannibal Valley*, the words
of a missionary who was in an airplane over Western New
Guinea.

> "As I looked down at the vast sweep of the valley floor dotted
> with villages and gardens, and beautifully terraced hillsides
> reaching up toward the rim of the mountains . . . my heart thrilled
> with the anticipation of our soon occupying the area. I was in-
> terested in the villages and gardens, but more than that I was
> eager to see the people. Most of them were in hiding but a few of
> the braver ones stood out in the open, watching the plane as we
> made our way up and down the valley. As these few came into
> view, I talked to them in my heart, 'You, old man standing there
> in the village compound, will have the opportunity of hearing
> the gospel. Like one of our Kapauku Christians, you'll be able to
> say when death is near that your family need not grieve. For since
> you have come to know the Saviour lives, someday you will rise
> from your shallow grave on the mountain slope to meet Him
> and them in the air.' . . . 'You, little girl, will find a place in the
> hearts and home as did Ruth [another pupil] and Marta and so
> many other Kapauku children. You will not need to fear being sold
> into a marriage that offers little more than a heartache. You, too,
> will know the Christ and come to find refuge in the shadow of the
> Almighty.' "[14]

All of this is accomplished not by theology, good or bad, but by
the gospel. For it is the gospel which is fruitful and productive.
It is the gospel which "prospers in spite of atrophy and distortion
and stimulates faith and new life despite expansion of churches,
despite rigid theology, despite domestic opposition to a church
or theology, and despite cultures and ways of life bound to particular civilizations."[15]

But the prevalent interest in theology of missions need not be an escape. It can be for the sake of an encounter and can lead to pressing forward into the world of the heathen. Indeed, if it is true theology and not an exercise in theory it will do just this. Theology is the church's interpretation of the gospel. It is reflection upon the great and fundamental themes of Scripture, the love of God, the Incarnation, the Crucifixion, the Resurrection, the Christian hope. Through it is reviewed, with the reviewer personally and deeply involved, God's seeking love and His purpose for all mankind. True theology is never an academic exercise; it springs from personal commitment and seeks new understanding of God's mission for our world as a means of sharing more deeply and more truly in that mission. Theology of missions is no separate esoteric discipline; it is theology which centers in God's revelation of Himself, in His mission to the world. Therefore, it is missionary theology. If God's self-revelation is kept at the center of our reflection, as in the Scriptures, our theology will be a missionary theology, a theology which compels us to missions, and will lead us not to escape but to encounter.

For encounter instead of escape there is needed a conception of missions which is true to Scripture. Some of the mission emphases in the Bible are referred to in the pages of this book. Brief attention at this time is directed to two themes: the world and the Kingdom. When these two are absent from our hearts, missions becomes a theory to be discussed instead of an expedition to be joined. Theology of missions ceases to be theology or missions when ". . . The world has almost ceased to be the *world* and is now conceived of as a sort of ecclesiastical training-ground. The kingdom is either confined within the bounds of the Church or else it has become something like an eschatological lightning on the far horizon."[16]

There is need for every level of the church's life to give serious attention to Wilhelm Andersen's statement: "If, in missionary service, the world and the Kingdom of God are no longer on the horizon of thought, if missionary witness is regarded merely as the connection-road between Church and Church, then there is certainly a failure to take into account all the decisive factors which must be reckoned with in any attempt to define anew the basis of the missionary enterprise . . ."[17]

Missionary theology requires moving out of ecclesiastical circles into the world. That suggests that the best theology of missions is never born in an armchair but in the world. The most creative missions theology is born on the growing edge of the church. Reflection on the great themes of the gospel comes alive and becomes fruitful when the Christian and the church stand on the frontiers of life, not in the sanctuaries at home. The requirement to go unto all the world points to the arena of the Christian's mission. There we are to be involved. We are not to act, as Bishop Newbigin suggests, as if God were interested only in religious questions. Our mission has to do with more than souls and the hereafter. Our arena is not a "spiritual" world of tomorrow but the present world created by God and filled with His children who do not know the meaning of His love and have no understanding of what God is doing in the world to work His purposes out. Christian missions need the dimension of the world, with all of its people and needs, to break the bondage of a church-centeredness which leads to complacency and boredom. Instead of speaking of "involvement" in the world and "presence" and other such terms let me use old-fashioned phraseology. When the church becomes sensitive to the existence of people, to the fact that there are two billion unevangelized people in our world today, to the meaninglessness and lostness of men without the Saviour, to their burdens and problems, then the church's mission and missions will come alive.

Missions also require the eschatological dimension of the Kingdom, about which more will be said later. Without this dimension we settle down into "churchification." Our horizon becomes filled with the institutional church. We lose our vision. We miss the spirit and confidence that come from knowing we have to do with the King of kings and that His Kingdom is everlasting. Our mission, however, is to proclaim the gospel of the Kingdom—a kingdom that has come and will come. We need the gospel of the Kingdom to give dimension and urgency to our task. Our labors are toward a future not yet realized, when the kingdoms of this world will become the dominion of Jesus Christ.

IV

Missionary Methods
Are Also Important

Let us assume that we have taken seriously the first three chapters of this book. Our conviction about the readiness of the world for the gospel has become a deep and dynamic conviction. We have preserved a specific missionary intention and specific missionary concentration in the life and structure of the church. Our theology of missions, or rather our missionary theology, has been reviewed in the light of the gospel so that we understand what we are doing and why we are doing it. Now our concern moves to the implementation of our missionary commitment. How shall we apply all of this to today's needs and opportunities in Christian missions? What can be said about our missionary methods?

Dr. Harry R. Boer has written: "When the method whereby the witnessing task of the Church is executed contradicts the nature of the task to be discharged, a working at cross-purposes ensues which can only result in failure."[1] Too frequently this truth is not readily recognized by those not involved in the development of missionary strategy and in the details of administering programs for overseas fields. It must be said that even among those so involved, the recognition of the importance of method is far too theoretical and often does not influence what we are trying to do or how we carry out our task. But when discussion turns to methods, Christian laymen, including some of the most enthusiastic supporters of world missions, will frequently express the desire that we finish as quickly as possible with such matters and get on with the Lord's work. We will make little progress so

long as such attitudes prevail. The Lord's work is vitally related
to method as well as to content of programs. For the character,
fruitfulness, and permanence of our missions overseas will depend, to a great extent, on how we carry out the task. The
method of work must not contradict the nature of the task.

It is not suggested, of course, that Christian laymen and the
home church are to be burdened and bored with debates on missionary strategy and with details of missionary policy. The home
church deserves more than that. It needs a sense of the thrill of
Christian missions and a vision of the vital world task of the
whole Christian community. But the home church must have
some understanding of what is involved in Christian missionary
outreach today and of what is at stake in our choice of a basic
approach in overseas work. This is necessary so that there will be
the needed support in the home church for a policy and an approach which have some possibility of aiding rather than hindering the goals of our labors. The purpose of this chapter is by no
means to suggest a new approach but to explain for Christian
laymen the reasons for an approach which has won an increasing
consensus among many of the great missionary churches of our
time.

Decision on approach, on basic policy, must be made in the
light of the nature of the task to be performed. The goal of
Christian missions is world evangelization. The proclamation of
the gospel of Christ to the unevangelized, the gathering of believers into the fellowship of Christ's church, and the permeation
of all of life with His spirit—this constitutes the world task of the
Christian Church. What method in overseas missions will best
contribute to the accomplishment of this goal? The answer: That
method which takes seriously the church of Jesus Christ in each
place, ensures the building up of the church, and recognizes it as
having primary responsibility for serving as God's missionary
community in that place. This is the hope for the evangelization
of large areas of our world.

An illustration will serve us at this point. If a missionary doctor
goes overseas to bring healing to as many people as he can, he
may accomplish magnificent results on his own. When his life-

work is completed, another missionary doctor can take his place, ministering in the midst of the population explosion to even greater numbers of sick people. The contribution to the improvement of health will be far greater, however, if, in addition to healing the sick, the doctor seeks to develop in that land a sense of responsibility for the health of its people, aids in forming an organization which will establish a program of public health, and contributes to training men and women in the arts of healing. Needless to say, these latter goals will dictate a method far different from that called for when a doctor concentrates only on the services he personally can render.

What we must be concerned about in Christian missions is not only the multiplication of our efforts and of our results, but the development in each land of a church which knows from its first days that it is God's missionary community in that place. Such a result will not be achieved by a paternalistic approach which does something *for* people rather than with them and through them, which infers that missions are our business, which makes all the meaningful decisions, which does not treat each church as a true part of the Body of Christ. We need, therefore, an approach which does not glorify the foreign mission but honors the church in the place and accords it all of the rights, privileges, and responsibilities which belong to the people of God. The character, fruitfulness, and permanence of our own efforts, the progress of Christian missions, and the building up of the Body of Christ are involved in the missionary method we choose.

In speaking of a basic approach in missions our interest is in the relation of the work done by a "sending" church to the church with which the sending church works in partnership in mission in a given land. Most of the denominational agencies, in implementing missionary outreach, have a relationship with a church in a given country, often with a church which came into being as a result of the earlier missionary activities of the mission agency. Partnership with an existing church is surely preferable to founding a branch of the American denomination. Further, in undertaking mission work today in a new field the sending church will almost certainly find a part of the Body of Christ, though perhaps weak and small, in existence in the territory. The major concern, then, is this: How does a sending "church" carry on mission work within the territory of a sister overseas church in such a way as to strengthen and not weaken that sister church in its missionary commitment and outreach? What relation between the two churches, what kind of partnership in mission, will accomplish most for world evangelization?

This matter has received great attention in recent decades. The prominence of this concern is an evidence of progress in Christian missions. The problem of relations with the younger church would not exist but for the fact that the missionary work of the Christian Church has led to the establishment of a younger church. One of the results of Christian missions is that new parts of the Body of Christ have come into existence in every part of the world. Their existence raises the question: When a new part of the Body of Christ has come into being, how does this affect the conduct of missionary outreach in that same area by another part of the Body of Christ, especially one which belongs to the same branch of the Christian family? The answer to this question is important; at times it is also difficult. What partnership will not destroy the missionary freedom and initiative of each body? What are the rights and privileges—for missions—of each partner? What arrangement will not undermine the integrity and selfhood of the "receiving" church and not hinder the missionary concern of the "sending" church?

Such questions have been the occasion of many studies on "church-mission" relationships. This subject received frequent attention in conferences of the International Missionary Council, now a part of the World Council of Churches. There appears an increasing consensus on a fundamental principle involved in such relationships although there are varieties of details in the implementation of this fundamental principle, which may be described as a church-based approach. The church-based approach is now used by many mission agencies, but it merits more understanding and support in the home church. Many Christian laymen fear that it is a departure from missions into interchurch aid, represents a retrogression in the purpose of the proclamation of the gospel in all of the world, and limits the freedom, initiative, and contribution of the missionary.

It may be helpful in understanding what we are moving from, what we are moving toward, how change was brought about, and the reasons for the change, if we look at the experience of one American church. The Presbyterian Church in the United States has had a great and fruitful missionary tradition. In terms of size, fruitfulness, morale, and achievement, its overseas program has been outstanding. Beginning work in many lands before there was any church there, its mode of operation has remained basically the same even after the establishment of a church, which has taken place in almost every field.

This mode of operation can be briefly described. The church's missionaries in a land are organized as a "mission." As the Manual of the Board of World Missions expresses it: "In every separate field there is a Mission, technically so called. It is composed of all the missionaries on the field."[2] The mission, then, consists of "foreign" personnel. It is fully organized, with officers and committees. It administers the mission agency's program in a land, making final decision on the placement of missionaries, final recommendations to the agency about the program, policies, and budgets on each field. The mission is autonomous, under the mission board. The program administered by the mission is vast and varied, including evangelistic work, medical and educational institutions, agricultural work, and such other programs as are considered important for Christian missions in any land. In that same land there exists a Presbyterian Church. It is also autonomous, with its own church courts and its own programs —such as evangelistic, medical, educational, agricultural. The mission and the church exist side by side, with many parallel programs, but each body is autonomous in its own affairs. The mission seeks to aid the church and to turn over to the church those mission programs which reach a certain degree of maturity and self-support.

The basic question for this mode of operation is whether, once the church in a land comes into existence, the mission should continue to exist as an independent organization administering an independent and parallel program. The continuance of the organized mission after the establishment of the church probably is due more than is realized to the persistence of precedent and to the fact that a pattern of long establishment is difficult to change. And it must be admitted that since it is always easier to "go it alone" rather than work with and through others, there is some temptation to follow an independent path. But such explanations are not fair to many missionaries who remain convinced that this arrangement is sound and that it offers the best hope for evangelization. Consider some of the arguments. This arrangement protects the autonomy and selfhood of the "receiving" church. That church is sovereign over its own domain. No missionary sits in church courts, to exercise his influence in determining the decisions of the church. This experience in self-government will be a great help in time of emergency when missionaries are withdrawn. This pattern avoids many of the dangers of a church-centered approach which can become absorbed in the organizational and institutional life of the church. It protects the freedom and initiative of the missionary, permitting him to labor in pioneering tasks in "regions beyond" while the church carries on its own program in areas where the church has been established. It provides the Board of World Missions with an agent on the field which makes decisions about the use of resources provided by the Board. These resources were given for the purpose of preaching the gospel to the "unreached." The Board's agent can ensure that the resources are used for this purpose and that a full accounting is given about the use of the resources. The home church will provide better support when it knows that its own missionaries are supervising the use of its gifts and when it is conscious of having personal ties with its own missionaries. These are but the major emphases in the defense of an approach which is used less and less in this period of developing churches.

However, in spite of these arguments it has been difficult to persevere in the use of this approach. In recent decades the independent mission, for areas where the church has been established, has been discouraged by conferences of the International Missionary Council and of its successor, the Division of

World Mission and Evangelism of the World Council of
Churches. Through these same decades the voices of some
younger churches have been raised against it. In the overseas
program of the Presbyterian Church, U.S., while the arrangement has been adhered to in theory, various concessions have
been made in practice as a response to current mission emphases
and the demands of many younger churches. For example, many
missionaries now attend courts of the church; at times they have
voting privileges and are even elected to leading positions in
church courts. Further, the majority of missionaries of the Presbyterian Church, U.S., are now frequently found not in the
"regions beyond," outside the territory of a court of the national
church (for this is increasingly difficult today), but working
within the geographical area of a presbytery, although not under
its jurisdiction.

Demands for change have been expressed in every field and
have led to constant discussion of this matter. It has appeared
that a conference on "church-mission" relationships is always
being completed, or is in process, or is the object of preparation.
In part as a response to the demands for a new pattern of relationship, the Presbyterian Church, U.S., called a Consultation on
World Missions at Montreat, North Carolina, in October 1962.
The purpose of this Consultation was "to provide guidance for
the Board of World Missions as the Board determines its philosophy and strategy for the years just ahead."[3] This meeting included representatives from the overseas churches, sister mission
boards in this country, cooperative mission agencies, and the
home church, and from each of the church's overseas missions.
Early in the planning there was determination that the Consultation was to be truly ecumenical. Those planning the Consultation assumed that all parts of the missionary enterprise had
something to contribute. It was decided to include the Assem-
blies of God and the United Presbyterian Church in the U.S.A.,
Bishop Lesslie Newbigin and Dr. Harold Ockenga, missionaries
and national Christian leaders.

> Some [delegates] came from churches affiliated with the World
> Council of Churches and some from churches which are not af-

filiated with the World Council of Churches. Some came from a
background of "faith" mission work and some from a background
of denominational mission work. The Consultation participants
represented varying theological emphases and differing views on
missionary philosophy and practice. There were young and old,
Christians from various races, countries and economic conditions.
There were Asians, Africans, Europeans, Latin Americans and
North Americans. All of these—numbering almost two hundred
—were invited to share in advising the Board of World Missions
on its philosophy and strategy.[4]

It was also determined that this would be a free and open
Consultation. Each invited group made the decision about its
representation. Such an arrangement produced expressions of
surprise from some overseas churches. They apparently found it
difficult to believe that a North American mission board did not
seek to influence the choice of representatives. They also appeared surprised that conclusions were not determined in advance. Careful work had been done in selecting the crucial
questions for discussion. Even in this decision, all participating
bodies were consulted and were given the privilege of suggesting
amendments. But no recommendations were prepared in advance. The findings of the Consultation were the product of five
committees which submitted reports to the general sessions of
the Consultation.

It is not surprising that the most difficult question had to do
with the pattern of relationship and mode of work. With most
missionaries on one side and national Christian leaders on the
other, the result was a compromise: "That the structure of relationship of missionaries to a national church should be worked
out by that national church in consultation with the Presbyterian
Church in the United States."[5] This recommendation, approved
by the Board of World Missions, led to a series of conferences in
which each national church stated directly to a committee
appointed by the Board the judgment of that church about the
pattern of relationship. Further, the Consultation had given
emphatic expression to the concern of churches on this matter
and provided opportunity for the Board to hear what the sister
churches were saying, which was: Missionaries should work within

the framework of the national church; the mission is a temporary structure and should continually move toward a reduction of its activities; when final decision rests with a mission there is danger of unilateral action; the mission should not have an independent program of evangelism; missionary assignment should be made by the proper court of the national church; primary responsibility for decisions concerning the Christian mission in any land lies with the church in that land.

The Consultation and the subsequent conferences led to change. However, in the change the missionary thrust of our participation has been preserved. We do not intend to center our concern in the ecclesiastical world of the younger church. Basically the change was from a "mission-based" program to what may be described as a church-based program. It should be emphasized that this does not mean a church-centered program. Christian missions must be focused on the world, not on the church organization. Missionaries are not sent for "police" action but to bolster the "attack" forces of the church. The energies of the sending church must not be spent in perfecting church structures, supporting the sister church's ministry, establishing central offices, providing pension funds, or raising salaries of officials. The goal of missions is not the organizational and institutional life of the church but the proclamation of the gospel to those who do not confess Jesus Christ as Lord and Saviour.

It must be admitted that it is this point of church-centeredness which raises questions about the church-based approach. Church-centeredness can develop. Aggressive evangelism can be lost through ecclesiastical machinery. The national church can develop a mind-set of "squatter's rights" in a territory white unto the harvest. Some national churches have fallen into the bondage of clericalism, which establishes an ecclesiastical domain and looks after it rather than after the evangelistic opportunities. If such a situation develops, the sending churches must say, "Here we stand. We must obey God rather than man. Our evangelistic duty must take precedence over interchurch relations." Such things must be said at times. Perhaps it would be helpful if they were said more often. We must not move from the dictatorship of a mission only to succumb to the dictatorship of a national church. But it must be said that all of the dangers of repressing aggressive evangelism are not on one side. American missions have also succumbed to ecclesiasticism. There appears as much evangelistic zeal among some national pastors as among missionaries. The national church is not seeking to deny the freedom and initiative of the missionary. This freedom and initiative have been allowed and guaranteed in every arrangement. What is insisted upon is the freedom and initiative which does not create a missionary empire, but fulfills what has been the great goal of missionaries, that they may decrease and the church in that land increase.

The new approach is not church-centered but church-based. Sometimes the approach is described as integration; that is, the work of the missionaries in that which involves the essential life and work of the church—evangelism, student work, Christian education, theological study—is made integral with the work of the church. In essence the church-based approach provides that the missionary contribution of the sending church is to be made through the program, within the framework, and by means of the structure of the sister church. No place is provided for an autonomous mission, although an organization for missionary fellowship and inspiration may exist. No longer are there parallel programs, but one program—the church's program, The church in the land becomes the base and channel of the missionary effort of the sending church.

It should be pointed out that there is only one basic difference —but what a difference—between the "mission-based" and the "church-based" approach. A field body which is the official channel with the home board—the body making decisions about missionary placement, programs, and policies—functions very much as in the past but is no longer composed only of American missionaries. It consists of a committee or a department of the church, in which missionaries have representation. The "field body" ceases to be a foreign group. It now becomes a church committee or department, composed of national Christian leaders and missionaries.

What is involved is far more than an organizational matter. Consider these words of Bishop Lesslie Newbigin:

> I have lived on the one hand in situations where the mission and the Church were two quite distinct and separate organizations with a total administrative dichotomy, and I have seen what seemed to me the inevitable results of that. The Church, so to say, took the hint that it was not the mission, and that it could therefore with a good conscience proceed to attend to its own affairs. But I have lived also in circumstances where there was no such dichotomy, where there was no separate organization called a mission, and where from the first moment of baptism new converts understood that being baptized meant being baptized into a mission, and that the first implication of baptism was that one went and talked to other people about the experience in Christ . . . that there was no other organization which would do this over his head or alongside of him or instead of him, but that this was what it meant to be a Christian. And I have seen in such circumstances the Church multiplying itself by a kind of spontaneous expansion, precisely because from the very first moment there was never any doubt on that point. . . . And yet I cannot help feeling that this total administrative dichotomy between two bodies, one called a church and the other called a mission, is in such flagrant contrast with anything that we find in the New Testament that it does demand a very critical examination.[6]

The reasons for the increasing consensus that such administrative dichotomy should not exist and for the increasing implementation of a church-based, one-program approach, are varied. The fundamental reason is theological—the nature of the church. In the New Testament there is one people of God in a place. In the Letters of Paul one does not find a "mission" and a "church." There is the one people of God which is a missionary expedition into the world in that place. The primary responsibility for the evangelization of the "regions beyond," as well as elsewhere, belongs to that people of God, not to a foreign group separated from the church even if it is working for it. In the very nature of the church the two groups belong together. This church-based pattern keeps the two groups together and prevents their remaining at arm's length. Now they must sit down together and talk together. They cannot continue side by side with no real involvement. They may become angry at each other but they can no longer go their separate ways. In the church-based approach the missionary and the church members and officials belong together and must live and work together.

The pattern of "integration" is more productive of missionary intention and concentration in the life and structure of the "receiving" church. The existence of a "mission" and a "church" does not lead to a church alive with missionary commitment but to a dependent organism. This is especially true in the light of the resources of the two groups. A "mission" has been, for the most part, the enterprise of an older sending church with vast resources of trained personnel and of funds. It has the resources for exciting projects and for all kinds of programs. Not much time will be required for the people in the area to discover where the exciting projects are taking place, where there are resources for new things. At the same time, often the church is weak in leadership and possesses very limited financial resources. The church is dwarfed by the powerful mission operating alongside it.

Perhaps an illustration will help us at this point. A large "first church" establishes a mission in a downtown area. That "mission" is after several years organized into a congregation, a church. Theoretically it now rules its own life, makes its own decisions, and carries out its own programs. But the "first church" continues its interest and concern. In order to aid the younger congregation without interfering with the church's life it establishes an independent program adjacent to the new body. Perhaps it builds an imposing structure for its auxiliary work, a structure much in contrast to the frame building which the congregation has erected after great sacrifice. The "first church" auxiliary "mission" has the resources of personnel and funds to take the initiative, to do things for the people of the neighborhood, to provide attractive and exciting programs. The young church will not grow in such a situation but will languish and become a dependent organism dwarfed by the benevolent organization alongside of it. This is especially true when it is assumed that the "mission" will operate on the growing edge of the church amidst unreached people while the church concentrates on Christian nurture and strengthening the organizational life of the church.

The church-based approach makes the program and contribution of the auxiliary body integral with that of the church, the people of God in that place. It preserves the freedom and initiative of those who have a special contribution, but preserves them within the framework of the church. It provides for a better sharing of those contributions because they are made within the structure of the church, in involvement with church leaders and members. It draws on the wisdom of all the people who are in that place for planning the best use of the total resources for the Kingdom's work. It leads to decisions which take cognizance of the church's understanding of the needs and opportunities and resources. The church that shares in decisions about programs will feel a deeper responsibility for the direction and maintenance of that program. The church-based approach does not provide for a foreign group to exist alongside of the church, doing something for the church or instead of the church or over the head of the church, but for missionaries to be "present with" the church, not working for but with and through the church members. It removes one of the obstacles to the indigenization of the church and its acceptance by the people of the area—a foreign group separate and independent and appearing to make all the vital decisions. Such an approach holds for all those programs related to the essential life and work of the church. There are other activities—such as educational and medical institutions—which are not necessarily conducted through the structure of the church but are church-related. More and more it is realized that such institutions may not be best administered by a court of the church but by independent boards of trustees. But these institutions are to be church-related, and the boards of trustees are to include official representation from the church. The institutions must not remain foreign, owned and operated by a group of foreigners. As long as they remain the property and province of an outside group, the Christians of the land will develop little sense of responsibility for them.

The missionary method described is the most effective means

of achieving the goal of world evangelization. It places missionary responsibility on the people of God. It plants a church which
will be God's missionary community in that area and beyond. It
develops not a "missionary's church" dependent on him and his
resources and often growing weak and disappearing after his departure. It is church-based and strengthens the church to be the
home base of missionary advance. It is in agreement with the
New Testament pattern of missionary work, a pattern for older
and younger churches in their missionary outreach. But implementation of this approach and fidelity to its spirit will not be
easy. There will be frustrations for the church in the land and for
the missionaries. There is always the danger of falling into a
church-centered mind-set and thus to dull the cutting edge of
missions. The national church can become dictatorial or hinder
missionary advance. The sending church will frequently be
tempted to "go it alone." It will be difficult at times to resist the
return, in practice or in spirit, to a pattern in which we make the
decisions and in which we do something for the Christian people
rather than with them and through them. Neither partner will
be faithful to the church-based approach without a good measure
of Christian grace and discipline and vision.

First of all there must be a concern for the whole Kingdom's
work. No sending or receiving church will follow the spirit and
method of the church-based approach if its primary concern is
for "our program" and for our denominational dividends. There
must be a dedication to world evangelization, not a selfish interest in credit for ourselves. The important element is that the gospel be preached. When this becomes the controlling aim there
will be less concern for "our" resources, our missionaries, our
rights.

Second, the success of this missionary method requires a trust
in the Holy Spirit. He works in national Christians and in missionaries, to accomplish the good of the Kingdom's work. The
Spirit also gives to both groups the commitment, insight, and
wisdom necessary for the best use of personnel and financial resources. The Holy Spirit does not work only through a field
body composed of American Christians. If we trust in the com-

prehensive work of the Spirit we will not need to insist that we have independent parallel programs, that the missionary body alone make decisions about the use of our resources. We have too much assumed that the Spirit must work through a mission for the wisest decision on placement of missionaries, budget requests, and selection of new projects and policies. But he works also through a department or committee of the church, or through a joint committee.

Third, the church-based approach requires a willingness to lead the "servant" life. The spirit of the servant must be found in all participants, in all members of the people of God in that place. All of the people of God, including missionaries and church members and church officials, must rediscover the vocation of being the servant. The one mission of the people of God in that place is the servant mission to each other and to the world. There is no place for insistence on rights and privileges or for any assumption that because one group contributes more it can control more. There is no place for the independent operator, the organization man, the dictatorial missionary administrator or church official. All must lead the servant life and work in the spirit of the servant. Only in such a life and spirit will there be found a way to give first priority to the good of the one Christian mission in that place.

V

Joint Action
for Mission and Missions

This chapter continues our attention to the methods by which we carry out our missionary commitment. The purpose is to consider how "foreign missions" are being affected and ought to be affected by some of the Christian developments of recent decades: the birth and growth of younger churches, the fact that the Christian community, and therefore also the missionary home base, is now world-wide, and the "great new fact" of this ecumenical era. We survey our missionary task in the context of the ecumenical movement. A secretary of the World Council of Churches was the principal speaker at a public meeting. In explaining his choice of subject for the address, he said, "I do not consider it my responsibility to talk about the World Council of Churches. There is enough institutionalism in the world already without any attempt to glorify this institution. My responsibility is not to talk about the World Council but about those things for which the World Council stands and which it seeks to accomplish." The purpose of this chapter is not to glorify the ecumenical movement but to focus on its contributions to Christian missions, on how the churches are working together to fulfill the missionary calling of the church.

Probably the greatest contribution to the ecumenical movement has been made by the missionary movement. This is due not only to the fact that Christian missions led to a world-wide Christian community but also because it was the task of the missionary frontier which helped to convince churches of the necessity of working together. As Dr. Harry R. Boer has written:

"If the ecumenical movement has anything at all to teach, it is certainly the unquestionable fact that the mission field has brought the older Churches to a serious re-examination of the brokenness of their situation."[1] This is but another example of the "reflex action" of missions on a church that seriously tries to preach the gospel in the world and to the world. Someday someone should write a large book on the changes which have come to the church as it sought to carry out its mission. The missionary task taken seriously has led to fuller articulation of doctrine (consider Bishop Lesslie Newbigin's emphasis that the doctrine of the Trinity was first clearly articulated when the church began to take the message of salvation to the pagan world), to clearer understanding of the role of the laity, to changes in worship and organization. The life of the church is affected when it takes seriously "that the world may know." It is not surprising, therefore, that Christian missions have affected the church's understanding of the nature and urgency of Christian unity. Some notable steps in cooperation were taken by North American churches as they confronted the home mission task on the frontiers beyond the Appalachian Mountains, in the Mississippi Valley, and in the far West. The churches very early developed that same kind of united effort in overseas outreach. The majority of early missionaries from the United States were sent out by a nondenominational missionary society, The American Board of Commissioners for Foreign Missions. A similar cooperative spirit was manifested in early missionary efforts from Great Britain and the continent of Europe. The London Missionary Society declared its purpose "not to send Presbyterianism, Independency, Episcopacy, or any other form of Church Order and Government . . . but the glorious Gospel of the blessed God, to the heathen . . ."[2] Unfortunately, this cooperative spirit did not continue untouched by competitive denominationalism.

But there was significant progress in cooperative missionary endeavor. Interdenominational missionary conventions provided fellowship and inspiration, followed by more formal conferences planned for consultation on how to evangelize the world. The first world missionary conference was held at Edinburgh, Scotland, in 1910 and led to a continuation committee which developed into the International Missionary Council. In the meantime mission boards formed organizations for consultation—for example, the Foreign Missions Conference of North America, with similar groups organized in Great Britain and on the continent of Europe. Comity agreements were developed to avoid competition and duplication of effort. There was desire to prevent confusion in mission fields and to ensure that great areas of the world would not be left without witness. There were further organizational developments. The Foreign Missions Conference of North America became a constituent part of the National Council of the Churches of Christ in America. The International Missionary Council was united with the World Council of Churches. For many American churches which are not members of the National Council or World Council, cooperative missionary endeavor is carried on through the Evangelical Foreign Missions Association of the National Association of Evangelicals and the World Evangelical Fellowship. It is tragic that so little communication and cooperation exist between the churches in the World Council and those in the World Evangelical Association, between World Council churches and non-World Council churches. With fellowship established between Protestantism and Orthodox churches, and with dialogue beginning between Protestantism and Roman Catholicism, a major task of the ecumenical movement is to bring into communication various groups of churches within Protestantism.

Such instruments of cooperation have arisen in response to a missionary situation. Their purpose has been strengthened by voices of younger churches affirming that the unity of the churches is an essential condition of effective witness and that it is imperative in the lands of younger churches. From some of these younger churches have come outstanding experiments and developments in the manifestations of Christian unity. The result of all of these efforts is that the churches are working together in many missionary endeavors. There are great interdenominational efforts in mass communications, such as the Radio Voice of the Gospel with its transmitter in Ethiopia. American churches carry on much of their ministry to human need around the world through Church World Service of the National Council. There is a united program in World Literacy and Christian Literature. Much of the missionary study material used in American churches is the product of joint planning through the Commission on Missionary Education. The Division of World Mission and Evangelism of the World Council coordinates efforts of Christians around the world in evangelism projects. The Division of Interchurch Aid, Refugee and World Service of the World Council serves churches throughout the world in making possible a cooperative approach to service projects in every section of the globe. These examples are cited from World Council circles. There are similar, though smaller, developments among non-World Council churches. Much is being done by churches working together to fulfill the missionary calling of the church.

But the end is not yet. More remains to be done. Churches have not yet taken seriously the ecumenical facts of life and have not yet shifted gears for carrying out the one Christian world mission. It is affirmed that the Christian mission and Christian missions in our time require "Joint Action for Mission." This phrase has become increasingly popular in top-level mission circles since 1961. A document on this subject was approved at the New Delhi meeting of the World Council of Churches and was commended for study by councils of churches. Its principles are having increasing influence and will affect the missionary outreach of churches which are related to the World Council. Our purpose is to understand what is involved and to point out three examples of "Joint Action for Mission and Missions."

The churches have been following "joint action" in certain projects for a long time. Some examples of these projects have been noted above. There has been a willingness to use an amazing measure of joint approach in relief work. Few denominations maintain a relief organization around the world. Instead, resources for relief are made available in the light of the needs and at the place of need. These resources are channeled through Church World Service or the Division of Interchurch Aid, Refugee and World Service of the World Council. The story in missions is far different. Perhaps this is because involvement in missions has a century or more of history, and therefore patterns of mission work have become fixed and traditional, while a large-scale and continuing relief endeavor is fairly recent. In missions we have consented to joint projects which have been exceedingly vital but have involved but a small proportion of resources. What is being proposed now is that we follow joint action for the total program in a particular area. Joint action calls for approaching the total task in a given area with the total resources available for all of the churches in the area. Resources include personnel and funds. The aim is a "re-examination of the use of resources in the missionary task of the churches in specific geographical areas."[3]

Consider some of the factors which encourage this new approach. First, at present we face the Christian task in a fragmented way. Take the Republic of the Congo, for example. In that land there is missionary outreach by several American denominations. There are also several British churches with their endeavors. Further, there are some mission agencies from the continent of Europe. In addition there are several Congolese churches. There is no total planning for the Christian mission in the Republic of the Congo, but only a piecemeal approach. Second, resources are available according to traditional historical relationship, not according to need and opportunity. A British mission society with very limited resources may be located in a fast-growing industrial area, while an American church, with ample resources, may be located in an area of dwindling population. One section of the Republic of the Congo, related to an American mission board, may be abundantly supplied with medical and educational opportunities, while a neighboring area may be lacking in primary schools. Third, the church or churches in a given area may be unable or unwilling to take seriously the challenge of a new frontier, such as ministering to college or university students. Fourth, since "the Christian mission must be carried on within and not apart from the structures of human societies"; since "the social structures of our time are largely impenetrable to sectional approaches by Christians,"[4] the evangelistic task cannot be met effectively by denominations acting as separate fragments. Joint action for missions would decrease the extension of denominationalism.

There is another major consideration in the joint action approach. This is the attempt to deal with a serious problem in Christian missions, the bilateral relationship between an older church and a younger church. So frequently it is a mother-daughter relationship. One church is almost always the sending or giving church. The other church is almost always the receiving church. Tensions develop. Conversation between the two churches often concerns relationship, not missionary advance. The younger church is often placed in the position of appearing to beg for more resources, while the older church is hesitant in missionary advance, fearing that its efforts may threaten the selfhood of the sister church. Joint action for mission is an effort to substitute a multilateral relationship between all churches in the area for the bilateral relationship between an older and a younger church. Consider the following statements of Bishop Lesslie Newbigin:

> . . . there is required the development of patterns of work in which the bilateral relations between missions and younger churches are supplemented and corrected by being placed in the wider context of a common planning for the whole mission of the church in a certain area. . . . It is hard for a relationship between two persons, one of whom is always donor and the other always recipient, to develop into a genuine and free partnership. The same is true in the relations between nations. It has proved possible for the United Nations to provide a context in which help could be given from wealthier nations to poorer without destroying freedom of partnership. The representatives of all concerned nations could sit round the table as equals, all potentially contributors and all potentially recipients of aid, even though some are much wealthier than others. Something comparable is needed in the relations between younger and older churches. . . . I have come to believe that some such development is the necessary condition for any significant advance in the Church's world mission today.[5]

It should be recognized that in that part of the missionary enterprise which is related to the World Council, joint action has

won wide acceptance, at least in principle. The Division of
World Mission and Evangelism of the World Council and
the Division of Overseas Ministries of the National Council are
committed to it, as apparently many member churches are. The
approach has been implemented in the Theological Education
Fund and is being used in the Christian Literature Fund. Proposals have been drawn up for joint action in medical work overseas and in missionary recruiting in this country. The administration of mission work in Indonesia through the Far Eastern
office of the Division of Overseas Ministries is on the basis of a
joint action approach.

It should also be recognized that we already have considerable
experience in the principles involved. For example, many denominations are involved in joint missions. A joint mission is a
limited form of joint action. For more than a decade the Presbyterian Church, U.S., the United Presbyterian Church in the
U.S.A., the United Church of Christ, and the Evangelical United
Brethren have maintained a joint mission in Ecuador. It was
early decided that it did not represent responsible stewardship
or sound strategy for each of these denominations to begin independent work or to establish in that land four separate
churches. The four mission agencies, therefore, formed a joint
board to administer a united program. Each of the four bodies
commits to this joint board all of the resources of personnel and
funds which it designates for Ecuador. Each body carries on its
total program in that land through the joint board. These denominations do not agree on all points of theology or policy. But
they have been able to work together effectively and to establish
one united evangelical church.

Again, there has been experience of the joint action approach
in Christian higher education in Asia. For many years the
United Board for Christian Higher Education in Asia has been
the administrative agency in this country for several Christian
colleges and universities in the Far East. As a matter of fact, the
United Board was originally created to aid Christian colleges on
the mainland of China. Today it has responsibility, for example, for Tunghai University in Taiwan and Yonsei University in

Korea. Some American churches engaged in missions in the Far East commit to this board resources of personnel and funds for a united approach to Christian higher education, while some of them maintain denominational colleges at the same time. Another example of joint action is in mass communications, with considerable resources committed to the Radio, Visual Education and Mass Communication Committee of the Division of Overseas Ministries. The spirit of joint action has also been very much at work in the relief program carried on by American churches. An approach similar to the above examples is anticipated in Christian medical work, to provide better medical programs and a few large medical centers which can carry on significant training and research programs.

It is not yet clear what a full joint action program will mean in terms of structure and organization. There may be developments toward considerable centralization, which apparently is thought desirable by some leaders. Dr. Truman B. Douglas, after visiting missions in the Far East and attending the New Delhi meeting of the World Council, wrote as follows:

> Must the churches go on forever running little bureaucracies on the order of the U.S. state department, with "desks" for each area and with secretaries at home or overseas trying to supervise the operation? Should not missions now become a work to be conducted through the World Council, in much the same way as aid is administered through the United Nations?[6]

Yet the Director of the Division of World Mission and Evangelism of the World Council writes:

> This [joint action] is not a proposal for a "super mission board" which would pool all the resources of missions and conduct global operations financed out of the common pool. This kind of centralization is sometimes suggested as the administrative corollary of the conception of the mission of the whole Church to the whole world. It would certainly be a mistake.[7]

There is, of course, the possibility of more organization. For example, when four mission boards create a joint board for work in Ecuador, the number of mission agencies is increased to five. But this ratio of increase would not necessarily continue. In fact, it would most certainly decrease in a wider application of joint action. And there is the possibility of no increase at all in organization. At the present time there is an amazing amount of missionary machinery. It would be interesting, and humbling, to learn how many mission boards and how much administrative personnel are involved at the present time in carrying on mission work in a particular area of the world. If there are difficulties over centralization this will not be the only problem. There is the question of confessional (involving denominational families) traditions, of the preservation of freedom for aggressive evangelism, of keeping strong the personal ties of prayer and knowledge and support. But there must not be attention only to fears and dangers. Attention must also be given to the advantages of joint action. The experience gained in joint missions and other cooperative endeavors indicates that the value of confessional traditions, freedom, and personal ties can be preserved. Of course, care must be exercised each step along the way, and new proposals must be judged in the light of their contribution to the growing edge of the church.

The subject of joint action affords the occasion for a word about ecumenical agencies. The move to greater coordination of denominational efforts may also be the time for greater coordination in the activities of ecumenical bodies. Missions in an ecumenical era are exceedingly complex. It is becoming difficult to distinguish projects of the Division of World Mission and Evangelism from those of the Division of Interchurch Aid, Refugee and World Service. Further, it is becoming increasingly difficult for an American church to know just what it is contributing to various projects. For example, the East Asia Christian Conference receives funds contributed through the Division of World Mission and Evangelism, through the Division of Interchurch Aid, Refugee and World Service, through United Church Women, through the World Student Christian Federation, and by direct grants. There may be other avenues. There is need for clearer and firmer delineation of channels between all parties.

We consider now three projects which are in keeping with a

united approach. An example of joint action for mission is the East Asia Missionary Support Fund. This project illustrates the spirit of the whole church facing the whole task in the whole world, with "redeployment of resources for more fruitful discharge of responsibilities in mission." This undertaking is sponsored by the East Asia Christian Conference, a continuing organization binding together the churches in that geographical area. This Conference is the best example of what is called "dynamic regionalism." It is also called "regional ecumenism." (A similar development in Africa has produced the All Africa Church Conference.) The churches of East Asia were the fruit of Christian missions from Western churches. As a result, the Asian churches had historical ties with Western mission agencies but few ties with each other. They did not know one another. The increasing consciousness of common responsibility and opportunity provided by their location led the Asian churches to organize the East Asia Christian Conference in 1957. The Conference is seeking to emphasize the ties which bind the churches of that area together and the responsibility of the Asian churches for mission and evangelism in their area of the world and beyond. It has been blessed with outstanding leadership and has made a remarkable contribution in the ecumenical movement and to Christian life and thought.

The East Asia Missionary Support Fund is the result of "Preoccupation with the task of evangelism" by the churches of East Asia. Those churches have sent out more than two hundred missionaries to labor in other countries, established evangelistic teams, placed emphasis on industrial evangelism and the witness of the laity. But the fact that "There are many times more people without a knowledge of God the Father of Jesus Christ in Asia than there were in the whole world at the time of Pentecost"[8] calls for thinking beyond traditional patterns and for bringing to bear on the evangelistic need and opportunity the resources of the whole church.

Here is the plan. Some of the Asian churches have more trained Christian leaders than are being effectively used in their own country. In Taiwan, for example, the number of students in seminaries and Bible schools is greater than can be used at the present time in full-time church vocations, although the church is growing rapidly. In Korea there is a large number of seminary graduates who are not serving in the pastorate. It appears that both Korea and Taiwan have personnel to share in missionary outreach overseas. The fact that this personnel is Asian, for work among Asians, offers tremendous advantages. There is further advantage in that the cost of supporting an Asian missionary is far less than the cost of maintaining a missionary from the West. However, the Asian churches can support only a very limited number of missionaries overseas. They have the resources of personnel but not of funds. To meet this situation the East Asia Missionary Support Fund has been established. The "sending" church (of Taiwan or Korea, for instance) will provide at least twenty-five percent of the expenses of their missionaries. What that church cannot provide will be supplied by the funds contributed by other churches around the world. American churches, for example, are asked to give $8,000 per year to this fund (with a maximum amount allowed from any one mission agency). Here is an opportunity to bring to bear the resources of the whole church on a great evangelistic opportunity.

This method of operation has advantages. It provides that all churches contribute to a common fund rather than for one American church to provide support for the missionaries of one Asian church. It is thus designed to avoid the bilateral relation between one church which is the donor and another church which is the recipient. It also represents an attempt to change the usual denominational pattern of missionary expansion. The missionaries are to be the expression of the evangelistic concern of East Asian Christians, not emissaries of a particular denomination. Here again is an example of the whole church facing the whole task in a geographical area instead of using a fragmented denominational approach.

This project of the East Asia Christian Conference provides opportunity for a word about missionary personnel. It is sometimes pointed out that the churches affiliated with the World Council of Churches are sending out a decreasing proportion of the total number of missionaries. Such a trend must be watched carefully and with serious concern, not only because of the need for world evangelization but because the sharing of life in missions is of supreme importance. But two considerations deserve attention. A church may judge, even reluctantly, that its most needed contribution at this time is not to send out an increasing number of American missionaries but to contribute half a million dollars to the Theological Fund or a sizable amount for radio evangelism. Further, the church may judge that its best contribution at this hour is not to increase the number of American missionaries (a large proportion of the total missionary force) but to enable Asian churches to send out missionaries to millions of Chinese in Southeast Asia or to other parts of the world. This would contribute to internationalizing the missionary force. It would also greatly increase the missionary force, for in all probability the cost of maintaining an American missionary couple would support at least three Asian missionary couples. Nevertheless, it is essential that American churches do not succumb to the danger of supplying funds while other churches overseas supply personnel.

A second example of joint action for mission is the Theological Education Fund, which consisted of four million dollars contributed by mission boards and a Foundation grant for a five-year program beginning in 1960: ". . . to develop and strengthen indigenous theological education, to stimulate local responsibility, to encourage creative theological thinking, and to provide a higher standard of scholarship and training suited to the needs of the churches to be served."[9]

The project proved so fruitful that plans have been approved for the continuation of the program, with a maximum budget of four million dollars, until 1970. Emphasis will be placed on strengthening the faculty, rethinking curriculum, a texts and libraries program, and other things vital for the training of the Christian ministry.

The Theological Education Fund represents a total approach to the needs of Protestant theological education in Asia, Africa, and Latin America. Resources have been made available according to need, opportunity, and promise. The ministry in a particular part of the world is not to be penalized, therefore, because the church in the area had historical ties with an older church of limited resources. The Fund is nondenominational, with the contributions designated for theological education, not for denominational projects. Sectional interests are subordinated to the good of the total task.

A final example of the whole church confronting the whole task in the whole world is the Mississippi Delta Project. This is in the spirit of joint action although not to the same extent as the other examples given. The Mississippi Delta Project is sponsored by the Division of Christian Life and Mission of the National Council, with the assistance and collaboration of the World Council. It consists of a program in fifteen northern counties in Mississippi, for the purpose of dealing with poverty and some of its causes, bringing relief to human need, and overcoming racial discriminations. It is more "mission" than missions, more of a service project than an evangelistic project. Yet it is similar to many endeavors carried on overseas by American churches which have educational and agricultural and industrial mission programs. And it is intended as a reconciling effort in the name of Jesus Christ.

This project is an excellent example of the new era in missions and symbolizes several facts about the one Christian world mission. The mission field is everywhere—in six continents, not just in three. The United States as well as Japan, New York City as well as Tokyo, London as well as Leopoldville, are in need of expeditions across the frontier of faith and no faith. There is no Western Christendom sufficient unto itself without need of help from other parts of the Body of Christ. In the interdependence of the Christian community, Christians can be "mutually encouraged by each other's faith." "To fill the world with the message of Christ, is a task beyond the power of individual Churches. And victory and defeat of the individual Churches in this service is the victory of us all and the defeat of us all."[10] Missions are no longer "foreign missions," with Western churches sending missions to "undeveloped lands." They belong to the whole church. The one-way pattern in missions (from Western churches to other people) is obsolete. Missions represent the obedience of Christians in the East and the West and they are directed to the whole world, for the mission field is everywhere and the gospel is to be preached to all nations.

American Christians find it difficult to be the object of a mission. But they can profit from the inspiration of a foreigner's obedience to the missionary imperative. They can be encouraged and aided by the faith of other Christians and strengthened by the Christian experience of other lands. The fact that other churches around the world help supply personnel and funds for the Mississippi Delta Project will give us a deeper sense of the interdependence of the Christian community. Further, this experience can illuminate for us the feelings of those Christians who are traditionally on the receiving end of missions. We will be better able to understand what it means to be a recipient instead of a donor. It is always easier to give than to receive. We are accustomed to give generously for missions. We have expected gratitude, and we have sometimes had doubt that the recipients of our aid were grateful enough. Now we may understand how difficult it is to receive. Further, we may be able to understand how difficult it is to accept "outsiders." The first reaction of American Christians, especially those in the South, was that conditions in our country were our own concern and not the business of others. A similar reaction in other lands has meant that our missionaries, with the best motives and plans, were not readily accepted, for they also are outsiders.

The Mississippi Delta Project in which we are the objects of a mission, supported by personnel and funds from afar, can help us in other ways in our own missionary outreach. We have listened in our churches to appeals based on a presentation of weaknesses in a foreign land. We have found it difficult to understand the feeling of foreign Christians that the worst features of their land were emphasized, that a fair picture was not given, that their country is not "undeveloped." Now we know what a humbling experience it is to have conditions in our country publicized around the world, to have "outsiders" talk of our poverty and illiteracy and discrimination. We have felt that if these conditions exist, the extent has been greatly exaggerated. It may be that this experience will lead us to more kindness in our own presentations and appeals. It may also contribute to a deeper partnership with Christians in areas where we maintain missions. One concern expressed by Christians in the South was whether there had been extensive consultation with the churches in the area, to determine the churches' understanding of the needs and of the best procedures. Evidence indicates that there was such consultation. Our concern should lead us to greater hesitancy in going over the head of a national church with which we work, to approve no independent programs apart from full consultation, to give serious consideration to the desires and judgment of Christians among whom we work, to strive for identification with the Christians so that we can work with them and through them.

The Mississippi Delta Project has the possibility of aiding the people in the area, of helping us to see how our mission looks to those in other lands, of providing the opportunity for Christians of various lands to share their Christian experience with us. It is a symbol of the new dimension in the Christian mission today which calls for going beyond traditional patterns.

These examples of joint action for mission give evidence of the vitality of the Christian mission and of Christian missions in our time. Churches are seeking together new ways to fulfill the missionary calling of the church. They seek the leading of God's Spirit in determining what are the next steps which need to be taken.

VI

The Incarnational Life

Overseas expeditions across the frontier of faith and no faith require some professional soldiers. We come, then, to consider the professional missionary and his part in the vocation of the church to press forward into the world of the heathen. At his best, the professional missionary has an important and dynamic role in Christian missions. At its best, his task is significant and challenging. It is a world task, a ministry in the world and for the world and world-wide in scope. It is international and interracial. It addresses itself to a universal longing—the longing for faith and for a faith for this one world—and rests on the faith that this world can be redeemed. It is a frontier task. The great frontier today is not geographical but across the boundary line of faith and no faith, and therefore it exists everywhere. The missionary is called to cross that frontier and to take his stand on some of the crucial spots and active storm fronts of our time—such as the rapidly increasing student movements, the slum areas of fast-growing cities, the circles of prevailing secularisms, the place of encounter with resurging non-Christian religions and philosophy. The missionary task is a revolutionary task. Its message, the Christian gospel, has been the most revolutionary force in history. That message of God's love and, as a result, of human dignity and freedom and equality has awakened the longings which lie behind so many of the current revolutions. The proclamation of that message, in word and deed, involves one in the mainstream of today's world. And the missionary task is a Christian task. It has an evangelistic purpose, accepting the deepest opportunity and obligation of the Christian faith—to witness to what God in Jesus Christ has done. It involves one in the "incarnational life"—to go to another people, identify with them, suffer for and with them, live the "servant life" in their midst, and offer oneself as an instrument of God's love.

All this is true of the professional missionary at his best. But it must be admitted that we do not find him at his best at the present time. According to the recent words of a mission agency executive, "Not many missionaries in the modern world are romping home with success."[1] This is an understatement. "Missionary, go home" and "the unpopular missionary" are a truer indication of the present situation. But such a condition may offer promise and hope, that the missionary may be once again found at his best. In the words of the executive, "In many places they are rediscovering that their function is . . . to be . . . little servants, insecure, vulnerable, acutely hurt, often despised and unheeded, just as Jesus was. But that is why they are there, not to be ministered unto but to minister and to give their life in whatever way the Lord shall ordain and accept."[2]

Missionary life today is a demanding experience. For the majority of missionaries this is not true in terms of day-by-day deprivations and physical suffering, since a large number of them live quite well. But they face serious trials and tensions. Take, for example, the fact that in many parts of the world there is great uncertainty for them and their families, and the frequent experience of being uprooted. A missionary moves his home to another land. In these days he may soon be uprooted from that new home, as has happened in recent years in Africa, in the Near East, and in Southeast Asia. The meaning of such an experience is reflected in the book, *The Chinese Ginger Jars*.[3] This is a wonderful story of a courageous couple who served in China until the Japanese invasion. For months they lived in a crowded repatriation camp. After World War II they returned to China and were stationed in a new area where there was a different dialect. They labored there until they were expelled by the Communists. They then began missionary service all over again in India and were again faced with a new environment and a new language. Experiences like these have been very common for many missionaries during the last thirty years of war and revolution.

Even apart from being uprooted there are exhausting demands. In many lands a missionary will live in an environment dominated by pagan customs or by great non-Christian systems of life and thought. These systems support values and practices contrary to what has been known in an environment influenced by the Christian faith and the Christian ethic. In almost every section of the globe there will be the daily sight of extreme suffering and abject poverty. The missionary will experience rapid change, social disorder, often the rigors of a trying climate, the strain involved in crossing the barriers of language and culture. He will often face a severe test in the prevalent nationalistic anti-white and anti-Western prejudices.

A part of the missionary's difficulty is related to the work he is called to do. In this new era of missions when he no longer is an independent operator or superintendent, his role is often not so clearly defined. His assignment may be one which in his judgment does not use to the fullest his talents and training and does not allow the freedom for his maximum contribution. The present missionary structures may appear, to an extent, to limit aggressive evangelism. The missionary may frequently work under colleagues who have less training than he has received and with equipment that makes his best service impossible.

One of the most difficult trials of missionary life is not being wanted. He feels the suspicion and distrust with which he is regarded by the non-Christian population. In all probability he will know that he is not genuinely welcomed by all church members and leaders. An extreme example of this is found in the report of the Christian Mission Activities Committee set up in 1954 by the State of Madhya Pradesh in India. "Conversions are mostly brought about by undue influence, misrepresentation, etc., or in other words, not by conviction but by various inducements offered for proselytization in various forms."[4] "There are, of course, many Indians—possibly even a majority—who still want missionaries in large numbers. They are mostly the inactive who are afraid of taking responsibility; or they do not want to miss the financial advantages which the presence of a missionary means to them or their Church. But these members are not really those who represent the Church and bear the responsibility for its life." "Our Indian partners . . . say: 'Every foreign missionary is today occupying the place of an Indian and does what an Indian ought to do; and that is not only true for the evangelistic work but for the work in schools, hospitals and seminaries. . . . Every missionary coming to India supports the denominationalism of the Western type.' "[5] On the basis of remarks like these— and in less extreme form they can be heard all over the world— we can understand the conclusion of D. T. Niles that in Asia missionaries are needed and invited but are not wanted.

The decreasing appreciation of missionaries is not found only overseas. In the Western churches which for so long have accepted the responsibility for sending out the great majority of missionaries, there is indifference, even suspicion. Apparently many Christians believe that missionaries have been outmatched in creative planning and alertness, outsped to today's frontiers, outlived in pioneering spirit. Many who have the conviction that we are not at the end of the missionary era acknowledge without regret that we are at the end of the missionary's era. The missionary is viewed in some circles as a relic of a bygone day, a noble figure whom time has now passed by. The title of the missionary has lost much of its attractiveness and glamor. From many circles at home and abroad there come suggestions that we find another name, such as fraternal worker. Even among devoted advocates of Christian missions there is recognition that if the name missionary does not need to be changed it needs "re-minting." There remains still an honor for individual missionaries—such as Dr. Albert Schweitzer or Dr. Paul Carlson —but considerable doubt about the missionary group. For decades the missionary was recognized and used in non-church circles because he was the major source of information about exotic lands and strange peoples. But that situation exists no longer, for thousands of international students, and American citizens with long experience overseas, are now available for programs here and there. Peace Corps volunteers by the thousands labor in primitive lands and receive credit for humanitarian services formerly rendered almost solely by missionaries.

Anthropologists, linguists, university professors, and government experts now swarm over the globe, and these add to the impression that the missionary after all is not indispensable and that his work perhaps is no longer vital. All of this is reflected in the increasingly difficult task of recruiting the church's best young people in sufficient numbers for missionary service.

This situation makes the life of the missionary very demanding. But there are other factors. A popular custom everywhere today, it appears, is to criticize the missionary. We have noted the tendency of many people to evaluate Christian missions first and foremost in terms of its faults. According to Bishop Stephen Neill, "To listen to missionary history as represented in some quarters, one would be inclined to conclude that missionaries had never done anything but make mistakes."[6] Of course, some criticism is deserved, but much of it is undeserved, uncritically accepted, and unwisely repeated. We have shown far too much acquiescence in unfair attacks. Among some Christian people at home there is the willingness to believe that missionaries never exported anything but Western culture. Some Christians abroad have been far too ready to believe that Christian missions have never done anything but serve as the arm of Western imperialism.

It is important to pause long enough at this point to affirm that it is time for Christian leaders to take up some defense of Christian missions and missionaries and in behalf of a fair and objective interpretation of the facts of history. Fortunately, there are some able Christian leaders today who are raising their voice in such a defense and in behalf of such an interpretation. Dr. Max Warren has reminded us that when the last word has been spoken about the "awfulness" of missions and missionaries, the whole story, or even half of it, will not have been told.[7] Dr. Hendrik Kraemer writes:

> . . . distortions cannot efface the fact that the Christian mission-
> ary movement represents one of the most amazing human phe-
> nomena in world history as a whole. . . . it is unique . . . by the
> power with which it has inspired and sustained through the ages
> numberless men and women to lives of devotion, service, danger,

loneliness. They were sensitive to the needs of the lowliest and most despised and downtrodden mass of humanity, faithfully persevering when often results or success did not ensue. . . . Christian Missions have represented for centuries the concern for the spiritual and bodily needs of the "unknown" and "far-off" neighbour . . .[8]

Bishop Lesslie Newbigin has reminded us:

On page after page of the history of Asia, Africa and the Pacific Islands, you will find missionaries laying the foundations for the cultural revivals of the twentieth century, reducing languages to writing, revitalizing stagnant languages, rediscovering the forgotten past of ancient cultures and creating a new pride in them, and protecting the living cultures from destruction. You will find them also in countless cases standing up, often alone, on behalf of peoples unable to stand up for themselves . . . [opposing] the exploiting of cheap labour by industry . . . and the over-riding of native interests by colonial governments.[9]

A fine tribute to recent contributions of missionaries is found in Han Suyin's book, *A Many-Splendored Thing*. There is reference to the many missionaries who after their expulsion from China by the Communists poured through the church guesthouse at Hong Kong.

In this room were the remains of a hundred years of missionary work in China. A hundred years of devotion, sacrifice and good works. For the glory of their God, in unselfish zeal; men and women . . . had gone to baptize the heathen . . . heal the sick, feed the hungry . . . In this room were the people who had worn down our traditions, broken our selfishness, awakened our social conscience, armed us with ideals, dragged our scholars from their poetic torpor and our peasants' superfluous babies from the cesspits, built our universities, our hospitals and our puritanism. They also had made New China. Although now we cast them out as instruments of foreign aggression, they have also made us.[10]

There is no reason for not admitting that missionaries took the gospel in word and life to newly discovered islands and to the interiors of vast continents. They served as instruments to bring into being a fellowship of believers in countless places across the world. They laid the foundation for the modern ecumenical movement through cooperative endeavor and by keeping before the whole Christian community the demands of the unity that we have in Christ. And they helped to keep alive in sending churches the knowledge of the readiness of the world for the gospel and the need for the readiness of the church for Christian missions. Their role has changed, but they continue to serve as reminders of the universality of the gospel which transcends the barriers of culture and race and language and nation, of the interdependence of all parts of the world Christian community, and of the fact that the dimension of the Christian world mission is to the ends of the world and to the ends of time.

Whatever admissions are made about his contributions, life still is demanding for the missionary, and this situation is reflected in his frustrations, disappointments, and personal problems. To an extent at least he has now become the object of the church's concern. It is increasingly recognized that his lot deserves and needs from the whole church a care that goes beyond commissioning him for service and providing financial support for him and his work. A beginning has been made in providing pastoral care for him as he labors amidst tension and pressures. More attention is being directed to the role of the national church, in whose area he works, for providing that care. It has been assumed for too long that "looking after the missionary" is a prerogative that belongs solely to the sending church. Now the church in the land of his labors is accepting more responsibility for orienting the missionary in his new homeland and in his new work and for making real to him the personal concern and welcome of the receiving church. Such treatment by the national church is demanded by Christian courtesy and in view of the service the missionary is to render in the land of that church.

Sending churches are also giving attention to improving a ministry to the missionary and to discovering new insights into the peculiar strains which he faces in a foreign land. A denominational mission agency has recently made available a report of "The Special Committee to Study the Pastoral Care of Missionaries."[11] The report reveals that in the last twenty-five years there were three hundred and ninety-seven "dropouts" from overseas service (in the same period approximately one thousand new missionaries were sent to the foreign field). This study indicates that at least in these years and for this church it was not true that once a missionary, always a missionary. Many of the dropouts were due to abnormal circumstances such as war and revolution. Some were caused by family situations or conditions of health which prevented further service on the field. It must be admitted, however, that "health," or the "demands of providence" are usually liberally interpreted and cover a multitude of factors, including a recognition that for some there was no longer a vocation to lifetime service in a foreign land.

The report estimated that one hundred and thirty-two cases out of the three hundred and ninety-seven could have been helped and perhaps saved for overseas service if adequate pastoral care had been available when needed. Some of the "crises" which require pastoral care were reported as follows: crises "early in the missionary's experience"; friction and misunderstandings among missionaries; frustration and disappointment with meager results; trouble at home; disagreement with mission policy; experiences during a furlough period in the homeland; adjustments between older and younger missionaries; misunderstandings with national Christians; problems related to missionary children; doubt. The first years of missionary service can be very difficult, with the rigorous demands of language study and all of the adjustments to a new culture. Even if parents make a successful adjustment they may find that their children do not. Small children are often disturbed over the loss of familiar playmates. Older children may experience severe problems in moving from a large grammar school or high school to a small "school for missionary children" where there may be but a few students in each grade. Trials come for parents and children if, as is often the case, a child must be instructed by his mother until he is in the fifth or sixth grade and then be sent away to a boarding school far from home.

Two items in the report may cause surprise among average church members. First, there are references to unsatisfactory personal relations with other missionaries. This is the more surprising in view of the deep fellowship that develops in a missionary group. Apparently, however, missionaries take out some of their frustrations on their colleagues. The report cites a previous survey which found that the greatest shock for one fourth of all missionaries responding to the survey was the friction which existed among missionaries. The strong individualism of missionaries and the fact that often they live close together, perhaps in a compound, may account for this fact. A second surprising item is the strong pleas for help in personal and group religious living. What is surprising is not the interest in personal and group religious living but the fact that in a group so involved with religious meetings and activities there should be such a consciousness of need for help in this area. There were many requests for retreats for spiritual enrichment, meetings for mutual spiritual development, worship services in one's own language, group sharing, Bible and prayer studies, and so on. The need expressed in many different ways was for strengthening the spiritual life, and the desire for pastoral care appeared to be a plea for spiritual revival. One cannot but hope that there will be future studies which will reveal whether there is any correlation between the friction and this plea for "spiritual help" and some conditions fairly common to missionary life: living in a compound separated from the great masses of people; a fairly high standard of living in the midst of people of abject poverty; submission of so many details of one's life to the vote of the missionary organization.

Enough has been said about the demands and tensions of missionary life. Unfortunately, more must be said. There is not only frustration; there is ineffectiveness. Far from "romping home with success," the professional missionary has problems and in a sense has become a problem. But the record of these men and women compares favorably with that of any other professional group working overseas. Some missionaries have become demoralized, lacking in an enthusiastic esprit de corps, and are no longer undergirded by a strong sense of mission or sense of direction. The fruits of their labors in our time do not appear impressive when one considers that there are 50,000 professional missionaries and that their work is supported by great financial resources and large amounts of equipment. The starting point for improvement in this situation must include more than the missionary. Our focus must be on the whole church. For one thing, what is involved is the missionary outreach of the church. Our concern is not simply the health and happiness of one group in the church—certainly not only with an American or Western group. The issue is the successful prosecution of the Christian mission and fruitful expeditions into the world of the heathen. Further, the focus of attention is the church because the source of trouble is in the church, not only in the professional missionary group. The ineffectiveness belongs to the whole body. The failures manifested overseas are the reflection of the values and attitudes of the sending group, not simply of those who are sent. There must be adjustments in the life and work of missionaries, but there must also be changes in the life and work of the church. What is essential is repentance for what we have made of Christian missions and a recovery of what it means, in Christian missions and in other aspects of the church's life, to be the servant people of God.

First, there must be a recovery of the true role of the missionary. Dr. Max Warren quoted one writer as saying that one of the greatest contributions of a missionary is to be the sand in the oyster shell. "Being the sand involves one in experiencing the sharp edges, the angles, and the tensions of the incarnational life, and then of facing the cost and involvement of bringing that experience into the experience of one's . . . brethren."[12] This is the true role of the missionary—the incarnational life amidst a "foreign" people. Of course, the essential gift of the missionary is his missionary faith and calling and his desire to share that experience. He communicates this gift through the incarnational life. This means, says Dr. Warren, being present amongst people, not so much going to people or doing something for them, as being with them, being available. The word missionary, he says, has the meaning in some languages of "the one who talks" and often has the connotation of "the man who is always ready to talk to us."[13] The incarnational life means being genuinely open to other people as people. The opposite of this availability, this openness, this incarnational life, is found in the missionary of whom it was said, "He really doesn't love us; he loves us only in the Lord."

The incarnational life means, in the words of the Reverend Théo Schneider, "To be there, on the spot, in a life-long commitment and a continued, sympathetic crossing into other people's ways, language and customs; to be there as long as circumstances, or revolutions, or synodal commissions or God himself allow it."[14] The true task of the missionary is, for the sake of Christ and as a means of witnessing to the gospel, in love to break through geographical and cultural barriers, the barriers of language and race and economic conditions and political viewpoint, to identify with another person and to become "profoundly available" for him. The task is to go to a person (not just to a people) of different race and culture and history and ideals and faith, to love him and live with him, to be present with him and for him, to live the incarnational life close beside him. This is the reason for the great emphasis on learning the language, for an able knowledge and use of the language is a means of communication and a symbol of the missionary's openness, availability, and identification. This is also the reason for the emphasis placed on service of long duration and deep involvement. There is a need and a place for the person who cannot serve for forty years. There are tasks that do not require forty years. But the missionary life at its deepest requires "presence" of long duration, for its purpose and goal is the incarnational life.

It is in terms of the incarnational life that we must evaluate the church and the missionary. And it is just here that we find our greatest problems, since any failure here involves the heart of our task. Consider three examples. First, we have lost something of the sacrificial note in missionary service. The missionary is not highly paid. His salary and benefits often amount to only eighty-five percent of the average salary of a pastor in the home church. However, it should be stated that the image of the "poor" missionary is largely overdone. There are many benefits—such as housing, transportation, medical care, and some grants for college tuition for the missionary's children—provided for the missionary in addition to his basic salary, which is quite low. And there is considerable security, often including lifetime appointment, in the paternalism of a mission agency.

But while the missionary salary and benefits are not large compared to American standards, they are far above the standards of the people to whom the missionary is sent. Often the missionary receives twenty or thirty times the income of Christian families in his new land. Frequently a missionary single woman will have an income several times that of a national pastor with a large family. It is recognized that standard of living is a difficult issue for the missionary and that he has agonized over it as much as or more than other Christians. However, he has also become sensitive and defensive on the matter and has constructed a good many explanations and some rationalizations. The health of the missionary and his family requires a higher standard of living than is necessary for those who have grown up in that country, and there will be far greater expense involved for the missionary in such things as the education of his children. Still, national Christians for the most part have not been able to see the element of sacrifice in missionary life. To them it means luxury. Many American Christians have been disturbed as they have sometimes seen large missionary homes, well supplied with food and comforts, adjacent to villages of great poverty. The problem is not only the great contrast, but is also the difficulty—almost the impossibility—of any deep involvement, any deep identification, and therefore any real communication of the gospel, when such a contrast exists. Some responsible Christian leaders of national churches have expressed concern to the churches of the West over the problem and its impact for Christian witness. They have called on missionaries to limit the amount of funds expended for personal benefits within the foreign land.

For the missionary and the mission agency this is but one aspect of a growing materialism which reflects the culture from which the American missionary comes. The missionary group can become more and more missionary-centered—but there are many missionaries who do not. The paternalism of the mission agency which provides so many things can lead the agency to forget sacrifice and can lead the missionary to expect additional benefits. No one has the right to assume that there is a unique vocation to poverty and that this belongs to the missionary alone. But the incarnational life involves demands which should be set forth as a part of that ministry for which the missionary volunteers. The sacrificial life, including standard of living, is a part of this ministry. Some recovery of the sacrificial note is essential. In some ways the church needs a new "breed" of missionary, perhaps more single missionaries, who can live on a more sacrificial level.

A second example of difficulty in the incarnational life is dependence on material resources to advance missionary work. Reference has been made to resentment against "various inducements" to win proselytes. It would be denied at once that any inducements have been offered. But then there are "the financial advantages which the presence of a missionary means." The American missionary has money, often supplied for his "work budget." This provides for his transportation and other things which are important for his effective service. But those funds often make possible the employment of "native helpers," or contributions to aid a church, or even gifts, sometimes "handouts," to individuals. The missionary often represents money. Sometimes the urgent requests for a missionary are not primarily for the gospel he brings but for the financial advantages he represents. Many a missionary has become disillusioned upon finding that he is sought out not for spiritual help but for material advantages. We must recognize that the absorption of the national church in money matters is in part a reflection of the large place money has played in our own efforts. Let it be said there is desperate need and magnificent opportunity for the generous contribution of American Christians. But those contributions need to be channeled in such a way that the missionary does not become a personal treasure chest, with all of the temptation this carries for him and for the people among whom he works. There will be more real advance for the work of the Kingdom when the missionary depends on the Holy Spirit alone for the fruit of his labors and does not run the risk that at least some of the "progress" is due to the power of money. In such a situation he may succeed less in those things which can be reported to the home church but he will be a better example of the incarnational life.

A third area of difficulty in the incarnational life is reflected in general standards and attitudes. Two examples will suffice. It is all but expected that American tourists will use the "free market" or "grey market" to secure the best exchange rate for the American dollar. This is hardly expected of missionaries, and is not true of many of them, or of mission agencies. Yet there are indications that this practice is widespread. Some missionaries do use the "grey market"—sometimes for personal advantage, sometimes for the "work"—to the disregard of the stability of the economy in the land in which they work and sometimes in disregard of the laws of the land. It is recognized that the legal rate of exchange is often far from being realistic or fair and frequently penalizes the missionary personally and in the work he seeks to do. Still this practice does not win respect from the merchants who buy American dollars or from the people of the country who know what is going on. A second illustration is suggested by the words of Barbara Ward: "Not all missionaries came out in the spirit in which fruitful cultural contact can flourish. Too much contempt for the 'heathen,' too much ignorance of alien cultures . . ."[15] As for general standards and attitudes, "Unless he [the missionary] stands out, amidst the low level of devotion which is all too common in the Church that he serves, by a conspicuous and recognizable likeness to Christ, perhaps he would have done better to stay at home. This is a formidable demand; but why should we not speak the truth?"[16]

It has been said that there must be a recovery in the church of the true role of the missionary. There must also be a recovery of the true significance of the professional missionary vocation. The vocation to missionary service comes to the whole church. It belongs to every Christian and roots in baptism, not in a special individual call. While this is true, there is an important function for the professional missionary. If he does not have a vocational uniqueness, he has a functional uniqueness. An example may help us at this point. A revolution for independence includes all citizens of a country. Each citizen is involved in the revolutionary vocation. But there are some citizens who while not having a unique vocation serve a unique function. They serve as a point of concentration for the revolutionary task and as a symbol of the vocation which is laid on every man.

This suggests the role of the professional missionary, and it is a significant role. Of course, we will be better equipped to carry on Christian missions when we are rid of the myth that the vocation of the professional missionary is the highest and holiest— but it *is* high and holy. We will be better off when we recognize the call and the contribution of the lay missionary who witnesses in his lifework. The overseas ministry of the Christian layman is of the greatest importance and deserves a larger place in missionary strategy and planning. But there must be no disparagement of the function of those commissioned by the church as professional missionaries. They represent in a special way the missionary intention of the sending church and its gift for missions in another land. They are a symbol of the missionary concentration in the life and structure of the sending church. Since the church's greatest gift in missions is personnel, not funds or programs, they are the symbol of the church's sharing of her life for the proclamation of the gospel and for the building up of the church.

It should be emphasized that the professional missionary does not include only those who are able to go for forty years or those who see clearly at the beginning of service that God is calling them to a lifelong term. The incarnational life depends for its greatest contribution in most cases on a service of long duration and deep involvement. Real identification in a foreign culture will require this of most people. But there is a place among missionary heroes of the faith for those who go for a specialized ministry for a briefer period. It must also be recognized that the professional missionary does not mean only an American or Westerner. As the missionary vocation belongs to every part of Christ's church so each part will be involved through its own professional missionaries. One of the tragedies and one of the greatest sources of trouble is that the missionary force has been so largely white, Anglo-Saxon, and Western. It appears that less than five percent of the Protestant missionary force comes from among non-white people. There will be great gain as the missionary force becomes more international and interracial and becomes a true nucleus of the Christian community of the whole world.

In any case, there must be a recovery of conviction about the significance of the missionary specifically commissioned for a full-time church vocation in the world. We will not be helped by depending only on Christian laymen who go overseas in secular jobs. The church must emphasize anew that in the prosecution of Christian missions there is a significant place for the church's missionaries and that there is a service for them which will challenge the best people the church has to offer. The church must not only rediscover the significance of the professional missionary; it must see to it that the missionary has the opportunity of making his significant contribution overseas. In this era more and more missionaries are related to a national church and receive their assignments through the church. That church, or a joint committee, can be just as sensitive to evangelistic opportunities and just as strong in a desire to use that missionary's contribution to the fullest as was the old-style American mission. The sending church must insist whenever necessary that its missionaries be used as missionaries and be enabled to make their missionary contribution. No church should permit its missionaries to be assigned to tasks which give them little scope to fulfill their evangelistic calling. Every church must insist that its missionaries be properly free for pioneering tasks on new frontiers, not necessarily geographical. The missionary's voice must not be silenced and the missionary vision must not be blinded. The missionary is an evangelist and must have the freedom to make his evangelistic contribution. The missionary passion which led him overseas must have expression.

VII

Crucial Issues at the Home Base

Much of our attention has been focused on faraway places. For our chief concern has been with "foreign missions." It is acknowledged, of course, that there is a missionary frontier at home, that the church must be present on that frontier, and that at home we must also be pressing into the world of the heathen. But at the outset we decided to concentrate on that growing edge of the church which is overseas. Our thought has been about the readiness (need) of the world over there and about the church's readiness (willingness) to respond with missions to the ends of the earth.

Now in this chapter we give consideration to the home front. But at this time our interest is on the home front as the home base for overseas missions. The situation at the home base of missions will have great influence on the success of our missionary outreach in other parts of the world. The amount of concern in the home church, the level of its commitment, the depth of its conviction, its willingness to sacrifice, its missionary purpose, will determine whether in missions we will provide a "patchy development, a little here, a little there," or go for the "big push." Consequently some of the decisive battles for missions to the ends of the earth will be fought in our own back yard. Many of the crucial decisions affecting the missionary enterprises are being made at the home base of missions now.

Because of the importance of the home base, considerable attention is being devoted to missionary education and promotion. It appears at times that far too much energy is required to keep the home fires burning. We spend considerable time and money in trying to "sell" the church at home on its overseas program. The fact that these efforts are not more fruitful is probably due in part to the church's realization that the aim too often is not "education in mission" but the promotion of financial support. Further, it is certain that all kinds of promotional efforts will have no lasting effect if there is lacking the conviction that missions have to do with the essence of life and with the essence of the church's mission. Education for mission must involve far more than information about missionaries and programs, and strange customs, and faraway places. It must be education in the fundamentals of the gospel, in the life and work of the people of God in our world today, in the fact that there is none other name, in the demands of the Christian mission at this hour.

Certainly education for mission must be set in a broader context than is usually the case. The following words of Bishop Lesslie Newbigin state the case well:

> Too often an intimate knowledge of, and concern for, this particular work has gone along with a shocking ignorance of the place of that work within the whole pattern of Christian witness in the area concerned and in the world. The foreign missionary interest, which ought to lift men's eyes to the widest horizons, can too easily become strangely constricted. Missionary education today, without weakening the special and personal links of knowledge, giving and prayer which have been part of the secret of the power of the missionary movement, must set them in a wider context, so that men and women who are accustomed by their daily newspapers to concern themselves with the affairs of all the world, may also be able to know what part the Church is playing in the life of the nations. The developments of secular civilization are compelling ordinary citizens to think in global terms. Christians who stand under the mandate of the Saviour of the World ought not to be less informed or less concerned concerning the cause of the Gospel in all lands than the ordinary citizen is concerning the course of secular events throughout the world.[1]

In many ways the possibilities in missionary education and promotion are greatly improved. There are new and highly efficient audio-visual aids. Missionaries are much more available through the means of rapid transportation. The presence of

Christian nationals and the recognition that they can aid us in a clearer understanding of mission and missions has made possible some very real gains. Just as Christians of the West can interpret to Oriental Christians the dimensions of the missionary opportunity in the East and beyond, so Christians from Asia or Africa or Latin America can help us see the dimension and demands of missions overseas as well as in our own land. Here is another instance where Christians can be "mutually encouraged by each other's faith." We can also be helped by the increasing number of church members who are visiting mission fields. A firsthand acquaintance with needs and opportunities equips a person for a special word in behalf of the church's outreach. But there is danger here. For one thing, the number of tours, caravans, tourists, and visitors is creating such a heavy demand on missionary time —and sometimes on missionary money—that missionaries are almost forced to become travel agents and entertainers. But there is another danger, that we will believe that if only the mission agency will become a tourist bureau or run a shuttle service to mission fields, using some of its funds to help along the traffic, the home church will be filled with interest in missions. If interest in missions means missions as a topic of conversation, perhaps this prediction is correct. But if interest in missions means a deeper missionary purpose, with a more sacrificial support of missions, then there is little evidence to support the statement. A visit to a mission field is by no means a sure way to arouse greater commitment or support. It may be the occasion for greater commitment in one person and for less commitment in another. A deep, abiding interest in missions at the home base is not developed by quick trips to faraway places. It roots in a deep personal experience of the gospel. If a person has been missionized, he will be a missionary and will support missionary outreach. This abiding interest is a product of conviction about the absolute need for the gospel. If a person believes that, he will not need a visit overseas to arouse his interest or sacrifice.

The depth of commitment to missions at the home base owes much to the "friends of missions." These are church members who "live" for world missions. In a former day, before the church accepted responsibility for world missions, there were those who formed missionary societies for the purpose of sending out missionaries and formed continuing prayer groups to engage in intercessory prayer for the missionaries and for the conversion of the world. Johannes Blauw has called attention to the fact that in the eighteenth and nineteenth centuries these "friends of missions" represented only a small proportion of the official church, which often was neutral about missions. He also believes that that church was more clearly manifested "in the much-defamed groups of 'friends of mission' than in the 'official Church.'"[2]

The friends of missions have their faults. Some of them apparently have no interest in the ecumenical movement and show small concern for manifestations of Christian unity. Little do they realize that they are thereby hindering the cause which they desire to help. Some of them also appear guilty of a strange inconsistency—they give no support to efforts to abolish racial discrimination, or they oppose those efforts. It is tragic that some of the most generous supporters of foreign missions are also supporters of segregation in the church. Such a situation is a sad commentary on our understanding of the gospel, of missions, and of the church. The friends of missions are also at times "unbalanced" in their devotion to the cause of missions. Some appear to believe that the church exists only for foreign missions, that no other cause has a claim on the church's resources until all the overseas needs have been met. Their narrow view of the role of the church makes enemies for the cause they love.

These friends of missions are far from perfect. For some, their enthusiasm and devotion have a strong mixture of pride, acting as if all the lost were over there somewhere, and of nationalism, a concern to use the gospel to protect America. Such positions are indefensible. But friends of missions are not the first Christians who have had blind spots and who have not seen all the implications of the gospel. In spite of these serious failings, they have been used, earthen vessels as they are, by God in His mercy. These friends of missions are burdened not only by the fact that some men are without bread but also are burdened by the fact that two billion people have not confessed Jesus Christ as Lord and Saviour. They are burdened enough for earnest prayer for the cause of missions. Some of them out of very limited incomes make weekly or monthly contributions to world missions; others provide in their wills for continuing missionary outreach. They have refused to become overwhelmed by the organizational and the institutional. They believe that the primary mission of the church is to the unevangelized. They make no peace with those who are neutral about missions. They have no patience with those who multiply programs and organizations for Christian people and show little concern for the unevangelized.

This minority group of "despised" friends of missions is needed in the church. It may be that when the history of the church in the twentieth century is written it will be said that the church kept alive her missionary intent and preserved a place of missionary concentration in the structure of the church, in part because this group opposed the neutralism about missions in the church. For there is much mission neutralism in the church. There is a tendency to succumb to ecclesiastical order in preference to missionary ardor. Always there will be those who become absorbed in ecclesiastical machinery or interchurch and intrachurch bureaucracy. The temptation is always present to settle for the lowest common denominator of mission interest. But friends of missions in every age have insisted that the church must not live for herself, that primacy must be given to evangelizing the world for Jesus Christ.

It is becoming increasingly difficult, in spite of the efforts of these friends, to keep before the home base in any distinct way the special claims of evangelism, whether at home or abroad. This is, perhaps, not due primarily to neutralism about missions or to any opposition to evangelism but to the pattern of denominational life. The denomination has a total program, and it must organize for that total program. There are many agencies and causes. It is important that all of these agencies work together for the total program of the church and not give the appearance of rival and competing organizations. The church has responsibility for providing the support which will make possible the programs of these agencies which the church deems necessary for the church to fulfill her mission. In the interests of all of these programs there is increasingly, and almost inevitably so, a move toward unified promotion and a unified budget. In such a unified approach one cause seldom receives more emphasis than another, except in terms of larger percentage of the unified budget. "Missions" may receive a larger percentage than "pensions" but both are items in the budget. In order that all causes may receive a fair support, there is emphasis on giving to the total program, sometimes poorly expressed as contributing to the budget. The local church member makes an annual pledge, knowing his gift is used for local, regional, and denominational programs. Having made his annual pledge he is assured that he will not be besieged with a multitude of special appeals. Consequently the observance of a "week of prayer and self-denial" has declined. There are still seasonal emphases for various causes, but less and less provision for a sacrificial response at the time a challenging appeal is presented.

This is not written in criticism. No one can study all of the factors involved without appreciating reasons which have led to the present development. And no one has the right to criticize who does not view with sympathy the efforts of the church to deal wisely with a difficult situation and who does not realize with great appreciation the gains for missions in a responsible denominational approach to finances. It will not be easy to discover any alternative to the present developments. But it must be recognized that missions, and to some extent its financial support, may be de-emphasized in this approach. Any loss of financial support is not to be compared to the harm that is done when missions becomes just one more cause of the church, when seasons of special corporate prayer and sacrifice for the unevangelized people at home and abroad are no longer observed or are not a serious part of the church's life. Surely there must be some way to keep prominent in the church's structure and budget and promotion, however unified they must be for the good of the total mission of the church, and to keep prominent in the minds of church members, the church's obligation to proclaim the gospel to the unevangelized and to extend the bounds of the Christian family.

We turn now to note briefly some of the great needs and great decisions at the home base of missions.

(1) The determination to advance the Christian world mission in a revolutionary age. There are many things in a revolutionary age which tempt the home church to lose heart. There is danger. As I write these words I am very conscious of the gains of rebel forces in the Republic of the Congo. One Methodist missionary has been killed, others have been captured. Rebel forces have been reported within one hundred fifty miles of Presbyterian missionaries gathered in the city of Luluabourg. Danger is not far away from them and it is threatening to come closer. Not only is there danger in a revolutionary age; there is also destruction. In the Congo uprising of 1960, much missionary property was destroyed or heavily damaged. Personal possessions were lost. Further, there is disruption. Evacuation of all missionaries from an area sometimes becomes necessary. At other times missionaries must be moved from particular places within a country. Families are separated, with the husband often working eighteen months or two years without his wife and children. It becomes difficult to preserve continuity of work or to carry out a planned program. There is no stability but instead much inconvenience. Transportation is no longer dependable. Sometimes there is difficulty in securing visas for entrance to a particular land. Supplies are delayed if not stopped altogether. And a revolutionary situation always has its political overtones. Anti-white and anti-Western and anti-United States slogans may be used. Some revolutionary leaders may look to Moscow or Peking. Such a situation leads to questions among mission supporters at home.

It is difficult to carry on mission work in a revolutionary age. One reason for this is that some church members at the home base begin to express doubt that we ought to make the effort under such circumstances. Some view the developments as proof that missions have not been successful. They suggest removing our missionaries and ending our work in the area of revolution. They question whether it is good "business" to continue our endeavors under such conditions.

But we cannot end our witness if there is any way to continue Christian missions. For one thing, such an attitude would soon limit missionary outreach to the safe places of the world, and these are very few. It would mean forsaking people in a particular land at the time they most need the "Christian presence." It would abandon witness at a crucial period in the nation's history and thus lose, perhaps for decades, an opportunity to make a creative contribution in the name of Christ. A minister once took his vacation far from his home state and was hospitalized for weeks with pneumonia. The minister's salary was not paid, for, said the church treasurer, he is not on the job. "It must be terrible to have to work under conditions like that," said a friend. "Yes," said the minister, "but it would be terrible not to be willing to work under these conditions." We may agree that it is terrible to have to carry on the Christian mission in a revolutionary world, but it will be terrible if we do not have the concern and commitment for just such a task, especially since the present revolutionary situation may last a lifetime.

The willingness to work under such conditions requires patience and fortitude and commitment on the part of missionaries. But it requires commitment and determination on the home front, an understanding that the Christian mission rests on the divine indicative and imperative, that it is not an option we exercise when conditions are favorable. A revolutionary situation tests the missionary purpose of the home church. The advance of world evangelization in our time will depend on whether there is in the home church the determination to continue full speed ahead in Christian missions even when conditions are not favorable and the going is tough.

(2) The dedication to show forth the power of the gospel in a world that is weary with words. It is an exciting experience to accompany a missionary on a preaching tour. Such an experience often comes to a visitor to mission fields in Asia, Africa, and Latin America. What is impressive is that in some areas, chiefly rural, of these continents one is never lacking for a congregation. Whether at noonday or at nightfall, people gather, perhaps chiefly out of curiosity, and there is opportunity to share a brief

and simple message based on some verse of Scripture. Sometimes the messenger is challenged by someone in the group. The hearer may express doubt that the preacher really believes what he is saying, or he may ask why we do not practice what we preach. He says in effect that he is weary with so many words. What he wants now is proof that the gospel will accomplish all that we claim for it.

There was a time when our missionaries could proclaim one message and Christians at home could live another without the great masses of the people of the earth, we assumed, being the wiser. But such a situation has long since passed. The conduct of Christians at home is a powerful factor in the mission of Christians overseas. Our life in this country does not go unnoticed by people of other lands. Correspondence from various lands and conversations with people of various lands reveal concern about four areas of our life. First, these people want to know why our home life is crumbling, if Christ is the answer, and if the gospel has power. They are not ignorant of our divorce rate or of our morals. Second, they raise questions about two world wars originating in Western Christendom. With our centuries of Christian tradition how could this happen, they ask. Third, they are hurt and confused by our racial discrimination. A Brazilian was not so much disturbed by the race riots as by the discovery that some of our churches are for white members and others for Negro members. He asked whether we worshiped the same Christ they worship in Brazil, where segregation in churches is not practiced. Fourth, they ask about our denominational divisions. The multitude of American denominations in Taiwan or Japan or South Africa prompts the question of whether Christ can unite all mankind.

It would not be difficult to point out some incorrect assumptions in these questions. In many cases, perhaps, the questions may not represent real difficulties for those who raise them. But they raise real difficulties for us. In the words of Dr. Eugene L. Smith, we cannot export what we do not have. We cannot show forth the power of the gospel if it has not been a power in our lives, in our churches, in our society. We cannot make a case overseas for the power of the gospel if it has not overcome some of our divisiveness, ruthless ecclesiastical competition, materialism, and prejudice. The quality of our life at the home base affects the strength of our witness overseas.

(3) The dedication to provide more resources in a day of greatly increasing costs. Missions are expensive. We have come a long way, an expensive way, from the time when the salary of a missionary couple was $600, for a single person $300, "except a little less for those going to Indian country (Oklahoma) and Mexico." Today the cost to train and send to the field a new missionary averages $6,000 for the first year, including housing, medical care, transportation for the missionary and his family, and language school.

A large factor in the increasing financial demands is related to institutions, especially colleges and hospitals. In the beginning of mission work in a country, primary and secondary schools were established. Later when governments provided public schools the church judged that its best contribution could be made through a college. An accredited four-year college is an expensive undertaking anywhere in the world today. Hospitals were often begun in spite of a lack of adequate equipment. But the day of substandard equipment in institutions of the church has passed. Such conditions bring shame to the church and are a hindrance to the Christian mission. Today there is a large number of Christian colleges and hospitals. The increasing costs are forcing a re-evaluation, long overdue, of institutional programs. Probably we are seeking to maintain too many institutions, some of which have outlived their usefulness. Further, there is need for a joint action approach to much of institutional life.

Regardless of any adjustments made in overseas mission work, expenses are mounting and greater resources will be needed. What is required is the dedication of the home church to share a greater proportion of its resources with the rest of the world. There must not be the assumption that overseas work has a special sanctity and therefore has a claim for preferential treatment. The need is everywhere and the mission is to the whole world. The fact that a project is located overseas does not necessarily mean that it is more deserving or more urgent or even more in need. There are times and places where the good of the Kingdom demands priority for the needs and opportunities at our doorstep. A congregation can hardly claim a record of good stewardship if it neglects the inner city all around it while glorying in its offerings for projects across the sea.

However, it must be emphasized that the mission is to the whole world, not just to our own doorstep. What is disturbing is the increasing proportion of church funds used for local programs, to the neglect of urgent needs in other parts of the world. Financial records of major denominations reflect a tendency to live for ourselves. In some major denominations contributions for "current expenses" have increased more than twelvefold since 1930, while contributions to overseas church projects have increased only fourfold. In some denominations twenty-four dollars are used for needs on the home front for every one dollar given for overseas work. It is not suggested that we starve the agencies which serve the church in this land or that we maintain a second-rate program at home while providing a first-rate program overseas. It should be expected, however, that we think of the whole Christian world mission, that the church show concern for its institutions in Asia as well as for those in Alabama, and that membership in the Christian community would lead a congregation to compare the importance of an addition to its church plant with the importance of a project for witness or service in Africa.

This matter of resources is exceedingly important for Christian missions. Mission agencies are experiencing financial difficulties. What is at stake is a reduction in missionary outreach or substandard operations in the name of Christ. Here again the battle begins at home. It is a battle which involves the dollar. It must be fought in stewardship councils and through denominational structures. That battle will not be won apart from a recovery of a sense of mission and missions and a rededication to the Christian world mission.

(4) The conviction to recapture and refocus missionary enthusiasm in a day of world religions.

The modern missionary movement has been a tremendous enterprise. It has evoked great sacrifices. It has achieved remarkable results. And it has been marked by contagious enthusiasm. When David Livingstone spoke of the smoke of a thousand villages, enthusiasm ran high. When we believed in "the evangelization of the world in this generation," enthusiasm was all but boundless. Consider an example of this enthusiasm from the period of Victorian evangelicalism in England.

> It was the great seed-time of Christian missions, and quite outstanding enthusiasms were evident in the England of that period. To take Cambridge as an example, we may think of the striking effects of the Moody Mission of 1873, not least in the subsequent calling of the "Cambridge Seven," and the fervour of which they were typical. We remember how, within three months of the news of Hannington's martyrdom, thirty-seven Cambridge men had made a prospective offer to CMS for service abroad if the way was open. Between 1877 and 1893, one hundred and forty offers had come from Cambridge alone to the Society, and of these almost one hundred had been accepted. It is interesting to recall that Handley Moule, the saintly first Principal of Ridley Hall, Cambridge, found it necessary at this time to write: "I find it constantly my duty to press urgently upon men the claims of the home field, so almost universal is the longing to serve the Lord in the ends of the unevangelized world."[3]

But this enthusiasm has now subsided. Today one senses a loss of momentum, a hesitancy, an uncertain sound. The disappearance of some enthusiasm is not altogether bad. Some of the enthusiasm was born of romantic notions. Its replacement by realism is good. Then some of our enthusiasm has been tempered by the events of our lifetime. The great and fruitful mission in China gave way to "the loss of China." There have been other setbacks which reduce our optimism about the missionary enterprise.

Another factor in the loss of enthusiasm has been the fact that world evangelization no longer depends solely on us. It never did. But there was a time when world evangelization depended almost solely, humanly speaking, on the Christians of the West. This is no longer true. The church has been established in every nation and has become, though small and weak, God's missionary community in each land. Young churches in Asia, the fruit of Christian missions, have sent out some two hundred missionaries. So missionary outreach no longer depends solely on us. And this, unfortunately, has had its effect. As long as we thought that missionary expansion depended solely on us, we could generate great enthusiasm. In a day of "foreign missions" we were enthusiastic, but in the day of the Christian world mission we suffer a loss of momentum.

But there is a deeper reason for hesitancy and loss of momentum. We live today in a pluralistic society. We come face to face with some of the great non-Christian religions. We have found untenable our former attitudes of complete condemnation and condescension. Unprepared to cope with the confrontation with world religions, we have to some extent accepted a false tolerance. Christians have been influenced by a widespread assumption that all religions are good and represent equally good ways to the top of the same high mountain.

The result has been a loss of conviction. We have become hesitant about the message of the Christian faith and the meaning of the Christian gospel. We have become uncertain about the purpose of Christian missions and uncertain in our missionary purpose. Theoretically we still affirm the uniqueness and finality of Jesus Christ. But we have become uncertain as to what this means in a day of world religions. Our sense of the urgency of Christian missions has been weakened.

The basic question is, do we believe that to man's need of Jesus Christ for salvation, there is absolutely no exception in the whole wide world? If we do not believe that, Christian missions will not endure. If we do not believe that, we have departed from the Christian faith, for the heart of that faith is that He is the only Saviour. And, of course, if we do not believe that He is the only Saviour there will be no enthusiasm for sharing the gospel with the whole world, no strong missionary purpose.

The matter of recapturing and refocusing enthusiasm in a day of the world religions centers in Christian theology. What is required is a recovery of conviction about the gospel. The recovery of that conviction is needed at the home base. Only as local congregations are renewed in the conviction that Jesus Christ is God's Word for the world will there be a sense of mission that carries us to the neighbor near at hand and to the neighbor far away.

VIII

Our Mission
Till His Coming

Our concern in these chapters has been the mission of the
church, the actualization of the dominion of Christ. We have
focused special attention on the segment of that total mission
which emphasizes pressing forward into the world of the
heathen. This is not the total mission. That total mission includes not only the proclamation of the gospel to more and more
people but also bringing them into the fellowship of Christ's
church and permeating all of life with His spirit. But crossing
the frontier of faith and no faith in order to communicate the
gospel to those who have not confessed Him as Lord and Saviour
is a privilege and responsibility which must never be neglected.
There is always the temptation to forget this part of the mission,
an outreach in love, because of the tendency to become institu-
tionalized and immobile, to concentrate on ecclesiastical order,
to be satisfied with the pastoral task apart from concern also for
the evangelistic task, to remain content with the edification and
sanctification of those who are members, to forget the growing
edge of the church. The church is always tempted not to care
enough to cross frontiers for those who do not know the Saviour.

Keeping alive our sense of mission and missions does not just
happen. It requires work and discipline. Some of this work and
discipline are in practical matters of organization, so that there is
preserved in the structure of the church the means by which the
church will be continually and fully confronted with the missionary task. But keeping alive our sense of mission and missions
involves more than organization. The best missionary strategy

will be a help but it will not guarantee a constant alertness to the frontier of faith and no faith. Alertness to that frontier, consciousness of the unevangelized, require a lot of caring, a lot of praying. The preservation of missionary commitment depends on inner spiritual strength in the member, in the congregation, and in the denomination. Such inner spiritual strength comes from a constant renewal through the remembrance of the missionary God who sent His Son, through meditation on the grace of our Lord Jesus Christ, through recalling the nature of the church and the purpose for which it exists.

This is to say that the preservation and rekindling of our commitment to mission and missions will depend to a great extent on prayerful study of the Scriptures, for it is in the Bible that we find the one story of God's love, the good news of the Incarnation, Crucifixion, Resurrection, and Return of Jesus Christ. Such study will not be limited to great "missionary" passages. It will involve a diligent study of all of the Bible and a disciplined hearing of what God is saying to us through the written word. The aid we will receive will not be, certainly not primarily, in terms of missionary strategy for our day. The Scriptures are no manual of missionary policy. They are supremely a witness to the seeking love of the Triune God.

In this closing chapter, let us seek help from Scripture. We will consider together a passage which happens to be a famous missionary passage. The main verse is Matthew 24:14, "And this gospel of the kingdom will be preached throughout the whole world, as a testimony to all nations; and then the end will come." The same text, with some variations, is found in Mark 13:10. You will note that the 24th chapter of Matthew and the 13th chapter of Mark are parallel passages.

The basic message of this text has been used in the title of this chapter, Our Mission Till His Coming. This verse, and the whole of the 24th chapter of Matthew (with the parallel in Mark), join together two of the great themes of Scripture, our mission and His coming. There is, of course, much material in the Bible, but there are only a few major themes. The covenant, the mighty acts of God, the Kingdom—these are some of the major highways which run from the first book of the Bible through the last book. There is also much in Scripture on the two themes which we are considering. On mission we read: "You shall be my witnesses"; "As my Father hath sent me, even so send I you"; "God was in Christ, reconciling the world unto himself . . . and hath given to us the ministry of reconciliation."[1] The followers of Jesus are told to feed the hungry, visit the sick, clothe the naked, and preach good tidings to the poor. Our Lord's last command was, "Go ye therefore, and teach all nations" (Matthew 28:19, K.J.V.). The message of the Bible is, of course, about what God has done, not about what we have to do. It centers in God's acts, not in human responsibility. But the Scriptures make plain that there are requirements of the people of God, that certain rights and privileges and duties fall to those to whom God has revealed His love. Those who are called by God are sent on a mission into the world.

There is also much in Scripture about His coming. To be sure, the Bible centers in the first advent and not in the second, as some Christians appear to suggest. But there is much in the Bible about last things, or, to use the technical term, eschatology. There is a definite and persistent and not insignificant eschatological dimension throughout the Bible which we too frequently overlook or refuse to take seriously. History is moving, under God's sovereignty, to an end, to a climax. The triumph of Christ at the end of history, His victory as the culmination of the historical process, is never forgotten or de-emphasized. His coming at the end of history inspires the prayers of His people, "Come, Lord Jesus!" "The Lord himself will descend from heaven . . ." There will come a "holy city, new Jerusalem . . ." The knowledge of God will cover the earth "as the waters cover the sea." There will be "a great multitude which no man could number."[2] Some of the best minds and hearts of Christian history have sought to interpret the meaning of these passages. The interpretations have been many and varied. But most of them have emphasized that history moves according to God's purpose to reveal the Lordship of Jesus Christ.

The joining in Matthew 24:14 of the Biblical themes of our

mission and of His coming does not make it any less difficult to hear the message of this passage. The words of the text were the reply of Jesus to a question of His disciples, ". . . when will this be, and what will be the sign of your coming and of the close of the age?" (Matthew 24:3). Our Lord replied that in the last days there would be war and persecution, hate and desecration, earthquakes and cosmic disorders, false prophets and false Christs. All of these things would constitute one sign of the end. There would also be another sign: As a prelude to the end and as a condition of the end, the gospel of the Kingdom will be preached throughout the whole world—and then the end will come.

Notice that in Matthew 24 much of the language appears to be strange. "The sun will be darkened, and the moon will not give its light, and the stars will fall from heaven, and the powers of the heavens will be shaken." It is difficult to know to what extent these words are to be taken as a literal description of future events and to what extent they are used symbolically. Then there is the word "end." What does it mean? Does it refer to the end of the world? Both Matthew and Mark state that "This generation will not pass away till all these things take place."[3] Moffatt's translation of the New Testament reads, "the present generation"; that is, the generation then living. It is interesting that some of the material in Mark 13 was used in Matthew 10 in the account of the sending forth of the Twelve. Some scholars interpret "end" as referring to the fall of Jerusalem in A.D. 70, while other scholars interpret it as referring to the end of the world.

There are difficulties enough in this passage. It is no wonder that in the ordinary congregation this passage is the subject of few sermons. It is also not strange that these words have been used by a few Christians as the basis of strange interpretations and of strange practices. There are those who use these words to set up a timetable of the end and to draw a blueprint for the last days. Most of us are familiar with a certain type of missionary who appears to discard so much of Scripture while clinging tenaciously to these few verses. They find here their mandate. That mandate is to preach the gospel. This means, they hold, word-of-mouth preaching. They find no mandate for Christian schools or hospitals or even for gathering members into congregations. Their zeal is for the coming of the Lord. That coming, so they hold, depends on the proclamation of the gospel in all the world. This means that all people on earth must have had an opportunity to hear the gospel at least once. Apparently, how real is that opportunity is not of primary importance. As these missionaries interpret the Scriptures, opportunity need not include instruction and Christian nurture in order to fulfill the one requirement for Christ's coming, that the gospel be proclaimed in all the world. Their task is to "sow the seed of the word" (not cultivate the seed) in every place, and then the end will come.

But there is more in this passage than timetables and blueprints and a mandate for an extremely narrow type of evangelism. The verse joins our mission to His coming. In doing so it forms a link with other New Testament passages. The Apostle Paul in Romans 9-11 teaches that the end will not come until the gospel has been preached to the nations and the fullness of the Gentiles has come in. In Second Peter there is a phrase which may refer to the same emphasis—"hastening the coming of the day of God" (2 Peter 3:12). And the book of Revelation (chapter 6) gives its picture of the four horsemen. There went forth a rider on the red horse of war, another rider on the black horse of famine, another rider on the pale horse of death. But these were preceded by a rider on a white horse. To this rider was given a crown, and he went forth conquering and to conquer. This appears to be the symbolic affirmation that before the disasters of the last days the proclamation of the gospel will take place.

With these other New Testament hints in mind, read again this verse, "And this gospel of the kingdom will be preached throughout the whole world, as a testimony to all nations; and then the end will come." As has been indicated, this verse links our mission to His coming. Consider, therefore, three results of joining these two together, three results of viewing our mission in the light of His coming.

For one thing, it sets our mission in its proper perspective, re-

lating it to the Lordship of Christ. Probably the greatest need
in missions today is perspective. Missionary circles are for the
most part marked by two characteristics. On the one hand there
is hesitancy, a loss of momentum, a slowly diminishing zeal.
Neither the certainty nor the enthusiasm which once prevailed
are now abroad. Many Christians wonder if the era of missions
has passed; as a matter of fact, they wonder if the need and
place of missions have passed. Such a mood results from discour-
agement and confusion. Difficulties appear on every front. Results are no longer dramatic. In places we are hardly holding
our own. The world revolution causes problems new and old
and leaves doubt as to the best course to follow. On the other
hand, there is frantic activity. Changing patterns and changing
world scenes appear to have outmoded many of the programs.
But new ones are invented or almost desperately sought, along
with new justification for their necessity. There appears to be an
obsession with what is novel. The frantic and nervous activity
may be a reaction of fear—fear about the future, fear about
what will happen to missions, perhaps fear about the continuance of "our way of life."

In both cases there is need for perspective. One is reminded of
the comment of Dr. James Moffatt, that many Christians work
for the Kingdom like those whose job is gathering wood for fire.
These people rush about frantically, fearing every moment
that the fire will go out. It makes a great difference, said Dr.
Moffatt, when in the work of the Kingdom we learn that it is
God's fire, that He will keep it burning, that our job is to stay
close to the flame.

It is this perspective about God's fire that we need about our
mission. We need theological perspective, that view in which
missions are related to and true to the basic truths of the Christian faith. It is theological perspective supplied in this verse
which relates mission to the Lordship of Christ. Bishop Lesslie
Newbigin's comments are helpful at this point. In missions, he
wrote, we become concerned about "something that we are to go
and do. It is even possible that we are already trying to do too
much! It is first a matter of believing, and of bringing all our

experience into the light of that belief, so that we begin to understand the world in which we live in the light of the lordship of Christ."[4]

The Bible, including the verse we are considering, sets mission in the light of the Lordship of Christ. It never lets us forget that we are serving the One who has come and will come. We are servants of One who became incarnate, triumphed over the grave, and will come again in victory. The mission belongs to Him. We are partners in His mission, not agents of our own program. We are not called to a world-wide effort for a cause in doubt. We are not charged to dedicate maximum resources in hope that we may carry a crusade to victory. We are not working for a Kingdom that depends for success on our frantic nervous activity and determination. We have not to do with a poor struggling cause whose success or failure rests on a matter of a few more cents or a few more missionaries. The future of that cause does not depend upon something that we are to go and do. The fire belongs to God and He will look after it. Our job is to stay close to the flame.

This is the perspective of Matthew 24. The words of our Lord in this verse are not an urge to activity but a statement of assurance. The statement is an indicative, not an imperative. "This gospel . . . will be preached." It is that certain. Our Lord said to His disciples: They will persecute you, hate you, even kill you. Many will fall away and most men's love will grow cold. Do not be discouraged. One thing is sure. No matter what happens, this gospel will be preached.

Such assurance comes when we set our mission in the light of His coming. This assurance was expressed more than a century ago by a great Presbyterian, Dr. Thomas Smyth: "What then though darkness cover the earth, and thick darkness the people! What though the idolatry of India still towers like its Himalaya Mountains to the unscalable heights of heaven! What though China repairs and rebuilds her mouldering wall of exclusive defiance to the gospel! What though Africa lies buried in the yet undiscovered mystery of her untrodden wastes! That darkness shall be dispersed, those mountains shall become a plain. Those walls shall be thrown down, and those 'everlasting' gates wide opened . . . The mouth of the Lord hath declared it . . ."[5] That same confident spirit breathes through the comment of John Calvin: "Whatever may be the contrivances of Satan, and how numerous soever may be the multitudes which he carries away, yet *the gospel* will maintain its ground till it be spread *through the whole world*."[6]

These things are true because it is Christ's gospel and because His triumph is certain. He will come on clouds of heaven with great power and great glory because He is the King of kings and Lord of lords. World revolution is subject to Him, not He to it. Closed doors do not stop Him, for He sets before us open doors. Again in the words of Bishop Newbigin, "He is the First and the Last, the Living One, in whose hand are the keys of death and hell. His cause is not in doubt. What matters is that we would know Him, know that there is none to be feared beside Him, none to be loved except Him, nothing to be desired beside Him; know both the fellowship of His suffering and the power of His resurrection, both His power and His peace, so that we may be the bearers of His peace to all the nations."[7]

Such perspective lifts our mission into a divine light. Mission then becomes more than activities and programs. It becomes other than a series of frets and fears. We find instead the certainty that can hold us steady in the midst of violence, bitterness, disappointment, and frustration. We find humility which recognizes fruitfulness as His work, not the product of our success. We are given the insight into purposes which will guide us in times of uncertainty and confusion. We will see more clearly the nature of our own participation—not to defend a poor struggling cause, not to lift it to victory, not to act as if it belonged to us, but to offer our testimony to the nations. We witness to what He has done and is doing. The issue is in His hands. This gospel will be preached. Our task is not frantically to rush about gathering wood for the fire in the fear that the fire will go out. The fire belongs to Him and He will keep it going. Our job is to stay close to the flame.

In the second place, seeing our mission in the light of His coming sets our mission in its true significance as a part of God's divine plan of salvation. The Kingdom does not belong to us and does not depend on us. But our mission is a part of God's ordained means for the salvation of the world. This is motivation for our mission. A motive which produced great missionary effort in the nineteenth century was the belief that those who had never heard of Christ were going to hell. While Scriptures testify that to man's need of Christ for salvation there is no exception, they do not speculate on what will happen to those who have never heard the gospel. And they do not suggest that the primary motivation for missions is that those who have never heard the gospel will perish. For Scriptural and other reasons, therefore, this particular motivation for missions has been greatly weakened. For most Christians it no longer has strong appeal. But there is Scriptural motivation which creates in us a sense of urgency—that God loves all men, that He has given us His Son Jesus Christ as the only Saviour for all the world, that He has given unto His followers the ministry of reconciliation, that our mission is a part of His plan for making known that love and that Saviour, and for witnessing to that reconciliation.

The recovery of this sense of significance for our mission is greatly needed. Oscar Cullmann wrote: "If the later Church has lost so much in vitality, if the workings of the Spirit, measured by those of the Primitive Church, are so very few, this is connected with the fact that this consciousness of standing as a Church in redemptive history's quite definite plan . . . has been lost or in any case greatly weakened."[8] It is no wonder that there is a loss of momentum and dwindling zeal and decrease of enthusiasm, if we do not have deep conviction about the salvation God has provided and about the significance of our participation in that divine plan of salvation. For if Christian missions represent no more than good activities which it is good for us to carry on; if they are no more than a pious form of foreign aid; if they represent no more than charity and humanitarian concern extended by the rich churches to the poor churches; if they are only the fulfillment of certain religious duties laid upon us; if they have not to do with the salvation absolutely essential for all mankind; then missions will not long claim the commitment and devotion of the Christian Church.

But missions, according to the Scriptures, are far more than this. They represent God's divine plan for world evangelization. The mission of the church is important. It is essential. This is due to the fact that God has acted for the salvation of mankind and has given to His church a part in His plan of salvation. This understanding of missions is implicit in the passage we are considering. Turn for a moment to the account in Mark 13. Whereas Matthew 24:14 reads, "This gospel of the kingdom will be preached," Mark 13:10 reads, "The gospel must first be preached to all nations." In Matthew we have a word of encouragement and of assurance. In Mark we have a word of responsibility. Mark interprets Jesus as saying: This is your mission, they will hate you and persecute you and kill you. Many will fall away and most men's love will grow cold. But nothing is to stop you. This gospel must be preached.

The proclamation of the gospel by human instruments is a part of the divine plan for the salvation of mankind. "God was in Christ, reconciling the world unto himself . . . and hath given to us the ministry of reconciliation." That ministry is not meaningless. We are not play-acting. We are not fooling ourselves that while everything depends on God we must play like everything depends on us. The fact of the matter is that God has given us a part in the full coming of His Kingdom.

We stand in redemptive history's quite definite plan. The mission of the church is a part of that history and is a part of that plan. As Old Testament people of God and New Testament people of God had definite parts in salvation history, so in the divine plan the people of God today have their definite part in salvation history. As John the Baptist was in the plan of God the forerunner for the first advent, so you and I are in that same plan the proclaimers of the meaning of that first advent and the forerunners of the second advent. As Paul was God's instrument for bringing good news to the ancient Greeks, you and I are His instruments for bringing the good news to modern Greeks, whether they live in Athens or Atlanta, in Taiwan or Texas.

Our mission is the consequence of Christ's dominion; it is also the actualization of that dominion. The dominion does not depend on us. The actualization of that dominion rests very definitely on us and on the church everywhere.

This responsibility for serving as a chosen instrument in the actualization of the dominion of Christ rests on every Christian. It is not an option. To be a Christian is to share in the mission. To be a Christian is to become a part of salvation history and to share in its plan and purpose. To be a Christian is to be a member of God's expeditionary force to prepare the way of the Lord. That preparation requires actualization of the dominion of Christ in every area of life. Every participation in Christian witness and service makes straight in the desert the highway of our God.

Oscar Cullmann points out that in early Jewish writings there occurs a startling question: Who delays the coming of the Messiah?[9] This is a question for the church today. Who by failure to proclaim the gospel as a testimony to all nations is delaying the coming of the Messiah? Who by failure in the actualization of His dominion postpones the coming of His Kingdom?

In the third place, seeing our mission in the light of His coming sets our mission in its true dimension, to the ends of the earth and to the end of time. The mission is to all nations. It is to the whole world. It is directed to six continents, not to three alone. The dimension of the mission includes the neighbor near at hand and the neighbor far away. The ends of the earth include not only places far away to American Christians, but also places far away to Asian Christians. It does not divide the world into "mission lands" and "non-mission lands." The ends of the earth include all people. Our mission is not to our kind of people or to those of our race and color, but to all men.

The home base of the mission is also world-wide. Participation in the actualization of the dominion of Christ is a privilege and responsibility not only of Western, older, and "sending" churches but also of Eastern, younger, and "receiving" churches. The great commission, "Go ye into all the world," is not an obligation that falls only on American Christians. It is as well an obligation of Asian Christians. It falls on all Christians. The missionary endeavor is not the privilege and prerogative of any particular section of the church or of any particular group within the church, such as professional missionaries. "You shall be my witnesses" gives marching orders to every Christian.

This mission is also to the end of time. It is in force until the actualization of the dominion of Christ becomes a reality everywhere—until He comes. We are tempted to have a far narrower view of the great commission. Our actions appear to say that our mission remains until revolution strikes, or is obligatory so long as the political ideas of a land are acceptable to us, or so long as the recipients of our aid show proper gratitude, or that it should command our allegiance so long as our missionaries are wanted and are appreciated. This is not the true dimension of the Christian mission. That mission remains in force for every Christian and for every part of the church. It continues in every place. It endures in spite of revolution, wars, persecutions, political changes, expulsion of missionaries, and closed doors. Its timetable knows only one stopping place—when He comes.

We have given attention to one passage of Scripture, to consider its message for our mission. This is only an illustration of the importance of continuing openness to the message of the Bible for our understanding of the mission God has given to His church. Listening to the Word of God in the Scriptures, and obedience to that Word, will save us from an activistic program of our own devising. It will deliver us from man-centered plans. It will provide the vision for our task. It will give us guidelines for participation in God's purposes. It will renew the commitment that will keep us sensitive to the leading of God's Spirit in these days. It will strengthen missionary purpose to serve on the growing edge of the church.

ACKNOWLEDGMENTS

CHAPTER I. THE READINESS OF THE WORLD FOR THE GOSPEL

1. Quoted by Max Warren, *Challenge and Response* (New York: Morehouse-Barlow Co., 1959), p. 131. Used by permission.
2. Max Warren, *op. cit.*, p. 131.
3. R. Pierce Beaver, "The Readiness of the World for the Mission," *Concordia Theological Monthly*, Vol. XXXIII, No. 1 (January 1962), p. 19. Used by permission.
4. Lesslie Newbigin, "Report of the Division of World Mission and Evangelism to the Central Committee," *Ecumenical Review*, Vol. XV, No. 1 (October 1962), p. 91. By permission.
5. D. T. Niles, *Upon the Earth* (New York: McGraw-Hill Book Company, Inc., 1962), p. 86. Used by permission.
6. Max Warren, *Tell in the Wilderness* (London: The Highway Press, 1959), p. 28. Used by permission.
7. Beaver, *op. cit.*, p. 19.
8. *New Delhi Speaks about Christian Witness, Service, Unity*, a report from the World Council of Churches, edited by W. A. Visser 't Hooft (New York: Association Press, 1962), p. 20.
9. From "Evangelism" by Bishop Stephen C. Neill, quoted by Hans Jochen Margull, *Hope in Action* (Philadelphia: Muhlenberg [now Fortress] Press, 1962), p. 84. By permission of the author.
10. Kenneth Scott Latourette, *A History of the Expansion of Christianity*, Vol. I, *The First Five Centuries* (New York: Harper & Row, Publishers, 1937), pp. 165, 167. Used by permission.
11. Barbara Ward, *The Rich Nations and the Poor Nations* (New York: W. W. Norton & Company, Inc., 1962), pp. 154, 15, 18, 142. By permission.
12. Beaver, *op. cit.*, p. 23.

CHAPTER II. THE READINESS OF THE CHURCH FOR CHRISTIAN MISSIONS

1. Stephen C. Neill, *Creative Tension* (London: Edinburgh House Press, 1959), p. 82 (footnote). Used by permission.
2. Lesslie Newbigin, "Report of the Division of World Mission and Evangelism to the Central Committee," *Ecumenical Review*, Vol. XV, No. 1 (October 1962), p. 89. By permission.
3. Walter Freytag, "Mission and Unity," *Ecumenical Review*, Vol. IV, No. 4 (July 1952), p. 409. By permission.

4. Manual of the Board of World Missions, The Presbyterian Church in the United States (1951), pp. 46-47.

5. Samuel H. Chester, *Behind the Scenes* (Austin, Texas: Press of Von Boeckmann-Jones Co., 1928), p. 53.

6. R. Pierce Beaver, quoted in Donald Anderson McGavran, *How Churches Grow* (London: World Dominion Press), p. 11. Used by permission.

7. McGavran, *op. cit.*

8. J. C. Hoekendijk, "The Call to Evangelism," *International Review of Missions,* Vol. XXXIX, No. 154 (April 1950), World Council of Churches, New York, p. 163. By permission.

9. Stephen Neill, *The Unfinished Task* (London: Lutterworth Press, 1957), p. 20. Used by permission.

10. Quoted in Egbert W. Smith, *From One Generation to Another* (Richmond, Va.: John Knox Press, 1945), p. 102. By permission.

11. Eugene L. Smith, *God's Mission—and Ours* (Nashville: Abingdon Press, 1961), pp. 83-84. Used by permission.

12. Lesslie Newbigin, *A Faith for This One World?* (New York: Harper & Row, Publishers, 1961), pp. 110-111.

13. Quoted by Hans Jochen Margull, *op. cit.*, p. 94.

14. Lesslie Newbigin, "Report of the Division of World Mission and Evangelism to the Central Committee," *Ecumenical Review,* Vol. XV, No. 1 (October 1962), p. 90. By permission.

15. "Report of the Advisory Commission on the Main Theme of the Second Assembly," pp. 23-24, in *The Christian Hope and the Task of the Church* (final section), copyright 1954. Used by permission of Harper & Row, Publishers, Inc.

CHAPTER III.   THEOLOGY OF MISSIONS: ESCAPE OR ENCOUNTER?

1. From *The Pressure of Our Common Calling* by W. A. Visser 't Hooft, pp. 14-15. Copyright © 1959 by W. A. Visser 't Hooft. Reprinted by permission of the author and the publishers, Doubleday & Company, Inc.

2. Quoted in *The Presbyterian Outlook,* Vol. 144, No. 46 (December 17, 1962), p. 3. By permission.

3. Lesslie Newbigin, *Trinitarian Faith and Today's Mission* (American edition, Richmond, Va.: John Knox Press, 1964), p. 31.

4. "Some Theological Bases of World Missions," p. 1. Prepared by the Board of World Missions, Presbyterian Church, U.S.

5. *Recommendations, Consultation on World Missions,* Board of World Missions, Presbyterian Church in the United States, 1962, pp. 7-8.

6. *Ibid.,* p. 31.

7. Hendrik Kraemer in a letter to Robert Bilheimer, quoted by Hans Jochen Margull, *op. cit.,* p. 138.

8. O. Michel, "Grundlagen des Denkens Jesu," *Evangelische Missions Magazin,* 1953, pp. 35-36. Used by permission.
9. TIME Magazine, December 28, 1962, p. 39.
10. Eugene L. Smith, *God's Mission—and Ours,* p. 83.
11. From "A Theology for Missions," by Nels Ferré. Copyright 1962 Christian Century Foundation. Reprinted by permission from the November 21 issue, p. 1415.
12. George E. Sweazy, "What's the Matter with the Presbyterian Church?", *The Presbyterian Outlook,* Vol. 144, No. 43 (November 26, 1962), p. 7. By permission.
13. Hendrik Kraemer in a letter to Robert Bilheimer, quoted by Hans Jochen Margull, *op. cit.,* p. 138.
14. Russell T. Hitt, *Cannibal Valley* (New York: Harper & Row, Publishers, 1962), p. 81. Used by permission.
15. Hans Jochen Margull, *op. cit.,* p. 67. By permission of the publisher.
16. J. C. Hoekendijk, quoted in Wilhelm Andersen, *Towards a Theology of Mission* (London: SCM Press Ltd., 1955), p. 38. By permission.
17. *Ibid.,* p. 38.

CHAPTER IV.   MISSIONARY METHODS ARE ALSO IMPORTANT

1. Harry R. Boer, *Pentecost and Missions* (Grand Rapids, Mich.: Wm. B. Eerdmans Publishing Co., 1961), p. 212. Used by permission.
2. Manual of the Board of World Missions, p. 33.
3. *Recommendations, Consultation on World Missions,* p. 3.
4. *Ibid.,* p. 4.
5. *Ibid.,* p. 19.
6. Lesslie Newbigin, "Bringing Our Missionary Methods Under the Word of God," Consultation Address, printed in *Occasional Bulletin* from Missionary Research Library, Vol. XIII, No. 11 (November 1962), p. 5. Used by permission.

CHAPTER V.   JOINT ACTION FOR MISSION AND MISSIONS

1. Harry R. Boer, *op. cit.,* p. 188.
2. Norman Goodall, *A History of the London Missionary Society, 1895-1945* (London: Oxford University Press, 1954), p. 3. Used by permission.
3. Pamphlet, "Joint Action for Mission," World Council of Churches, Geneva, 1962, p. 3.
4. *Ibid.,* p. 4.
5. Lesslie Newbigin, *A Faith for This One World?,* pp. 117-118.
6. From "Afterthoughts on New Delhi," by Truman B. Douglass. Copyright 1962 Christian Century Foundation. Reprinted by permission from the February 14 issue, p. 191.

7. Lesslie Newbigin, *A Faith for This One World?*, p. 116.
8. Pamphlet, "EACC" (East Asia Christian Conference) (no place or date), p. 8.
9. "Resolution Made by the Commission on World Mission and Evangelism of the World Council concerning the Theological Education Fund," Mexico City, December 1963, p. 1.
10. W. Freytag, "Vom Sinn der Weltmission," *Evangelische Missions Magazin*, 1950, p. 75. Used by permission.

CHAPTER VI.   THE INCARNATIONAL LIFE

1. "The Foreign Missionary Today," by Douglas Webster, in *Theology Today*, January 1960, p. 511. Quoted by Eugene L. Smith, "This High Calling," in *Occasional Bulletin* from the Missionary Research Library, Vol. XIV, No. 11 (November 1963), p. 4. Used by permission.
2. *Ibid.*
3. Myra Scovel, *The Chinese Ginger Jars* (New York: Harper & Row, Publishers, 1962).
4. Blaise Levai, editor, *Revolution in Missions*, Second Edition (Calcutta, India: YMCA Publishing House, 1958), p. 200. (From the Madhya Pradesh Report on Missionary Activity.) Used by permission of the publishers.
5. *Ibid.*, pp. 62, 65, 67. (From the section by Gunther Schultz, "Partnership in Obedience: An Appraisal.")
6. Stephen Neill, *Creative Tension*, p. 74.
7. Max Warren, *Tell in the Wilderness*, p. 27.
8. From *World Cultures and World Religions* by Hendrik Kraemer, pp. 86-87. © 1960 Hendrik Kraemer. The Westminster Press. By permission.
9. Lesslie Newbigin, *A Faith for This One World?*, pp. 107-108.
10. Quoted in Hendrik Kraemer, *op. cit.*, p. 97.
11. "Report to the Board of World Missions, Presbyterian Church in the United States, of the Special Committee Appointed to Study the Pastoral Care of Missionaries," 1964.
12. Max Warren, *Tell in the Wilderness*, p. 53. See also Max Warren, *Challenge and Response*, p. 73f.
13. Max Warren, *Tell in the Wilderness*, pp. 75-76.
14. Théo Schneider, "Crossing Frontiers," *The International Review of Missions*, Vol. L, No. 199 (July 1961), p. 319. By permission.
15. Barbara Ward, *op. cit.*, p. 113.
16. Stephen Neill, *The Unfinished Task*, p. 141.

CHAPTER VII.   CRUCIAL ISSUES AT THE HOME BASE

1. Lesslie Newbigin, *A Faith for This One World?*, p. 114.

2. From *The Missionary Nature of the Church* by Johannes Blauw, p. 113. Copyright 1962. McGraw-Hill Book Company. Used by permission.
3. John Poulton, "Like Father, Like Son," *The International Review of Missions*, Vol. L, No. 199 (July 1961), p. 299. By permission.

CHAPTER VIII.   OUR MISSION TILL HIS COMING

1. Acts 1:8; John 20:21 (K.J.V.); 2 Corinthians 5:19 and 18 (K.J.V.).
2. Revelation 22:20; 1 Thessalonians 4:16; Revelation 21:2; Isaiah 11:9; Revelation 7:9.
3. Matthew 24:34; cf. Mark 13:30.
4. Lesslie Newbigin and others, *A Decisive Hour for the Christian Mission* (London: SCM Press Ltd., 1960), p. 18. By permission.
5. *Complete Works of Rev. Thomas Smyth, D.D.*, edited by Rev. J. William Flinn, D.D. (Philadelphia: Presbyterian Board of Publication, 1857; reprinted by the R. L. Bryan Company, Columbia, S. C., 1910), Vol. VII, p. 33.
6. John Calvin, *Commentary on a Harmony of the Evangelists*, Vol. III (Grand Rapids, Mich.: Wm. B. Eerdmans Publishing Co., 1949), pp. 128-129. Used by permission.
7. Lesslie Newbigin, *Is Christ Divided? A Plea for Christian Unity in a Revolutionary Age* (Grand Rapids, Mich.: Wm. B. Eerdmans Publishing Co., 1961), p. 41.
8. From *Christ and Time*, by Oscar Cullmann (Revised Edition), p. 144. Copyright © 1964, W. L. Jenkins. The Westminster Press. Used by permission.
9. *Ibid.*, p. 159.

LIBRARY
JUNIOR COLLEGE DISTRICT
ST. LOUIS, MO.

INVENTORY 74

JAN 1 2 1978

INVENTORY 1983